Praise for *Kiss* **Your Customer** & Books/Programs by **Andy Masters**

"Ah, a book that combines business and romance! Just like in the movie *Jerry Maguire* when Dorothy (Renee Zellweger) says to Jerry (Tom Cruise), "You had me at Hello," Andy's book had me with the title. Then I opened the book and read one entertaining chapter after another. This book is filled with wisdom, tactics and strategies to build better business relationships—and is a FUN book to read. My advice is to get it, read it, take notes and DO IT!"
> **– Shep Hyken,** author of *Wall Street Journal* and *USA Today* bestselling book *The Cult of the Customer*

"Dave Barry meets Harvey Mackay in the most clever and entertaining business book I have read in years. Laugh. Cry. Improve as a person. Improve your business. A business humor masterpiece! Well done."
> **– Peter Fogel,** author and humorist, as seen on *HBO*, *MTV*, and *Comedy Central*

"Wow. If you can't relate to Andy's stories—you've never been in business, and you've never had a date! I LOVED THIS BOOK. Wonderfully written. It's simultaneous training and a comedic morale boost for your entire staff."
> **– Zelda Greenberg,** award-winning entrepreneur and author of *The Art of Bouncing Back*

"Andy offers a FUN, FRESH way to increase your sales, and improve every personal and business relationship."
> **–Randy Gage,** International Prosperity Guru, and author of *Why You're Dumb, Sick, & Broke...and How To Get Smart, Healthy, And Rich*

"I recommend Andy Masters' book as a good kick in the pants. It will help you get practical and produce results!"
> **– Po Bronson,** author of *What Should I Do With My Life*, #1 *New York Times* Bestseller, on Andy's debut book *Life After College*

"Andy presented at our 2007 Jaycees National Convention, and he was one of the best speakers we have ever had. His energy, humor, and real-life examples grabbed our audience, while providing specific strategies that our members could apply to improve their chapters and their lives immediately."
–Matt Booth, Chairperson
National Training Task Force, United States Jaycees

"Andy Masters was TERRIFIC — Fun, interactive, upbeat, and right on target with taking us back to the basics of GREAT human interaction — Face to face connections, and making a difference each day for yourself and others."
–Bonnie Cunningham, Meeting & Event Services
Price Waterhouse Coopers, LLP, and Director, Monthly
Programs New York–Westfield Chapter of MPI

"I have organized programs for the Women's Council of Realtors for 3 years. You won my award, HANDS DOWN, for the best speaker we have ever had!"
–Barbara Keathley, Past-President
Missouri Women's Council of Realtors

"Andy, you connected so well with our Young Business Professionals. You were energetic, motivating and down to earth. You would be a huge asset to any group who is looking for an AMAZING, one-of-a-kind speaker!"
– Consuelo Inestrosa, Event Organizer
Young Business Professionals of Boca Raton

"Andy Masters will add energy, content, and passion to your professional development event. Andy has the experience and skills to keynote or conduct breakout sessions, including workshops and seminars. His content is fresh, relevant, and timely in every way imaginable. BOOK HIM for your next event."
– Wofford O'Sullivan
South Carolina Department of Education,
after Andy's keynote program for 2,000+ attendees
at the 2009 Education and Business Summit

Kiss Your Customers!!

~ Andy Mark

Kiss YOUR CUSTOMER

77 REASONS WHY

Sales & Service
ARE JUST LIKE
Dating & Relationships

Kiss Your Customer
77 Reasons Why Sales & Service Are Just Like Dating & Relationships
By Andy Masters

Published by:
Hawthorn Publishing
U.S.A.

www.Andy-Masters.com

Printed in the United States of America
9 8 7 6 5 4 3 2 1

Book Design – Sue Sylvia   www.StaircasePressDesign.com

Library of Congress Control Number: 2009910331
ISBN: 978-09754610-9-9
Masters, Andy
Kiss Your Customer:
77 Reasons Why Sales & Service Are Just Like Dating & Relationships / Andy Masters.—
1st ed.

Kiss YOUR CUSTOMER

77 REASONS WHY

Sales & Service
ARE JUST LIKE
Dating & Relationships

ANDY MASTERS { AUTHOR SPEAKER FUNNYMAN

FIRST EDITION

HAWTHORN PUBLISHING

U. S. A.

About the Author

ANDY MASTERS

Andy Masters is a professional author, speaker, and business humorist who presents entertaining programs on a variety of sales, service, and work-life balance topics. Andy gained experience in a variety of sales, marketing, and management positions across several industries, before escaping the corporate world just in time to preserve his sanity. He also has extensive experience in the world of dating, though not necessarily successful.

Andy has written three previous books, including *Life After College: What to Expect and How to Succeed in Your Career*, which helps young professionals in areas such as networking, time management, and how to avoid being arrested at the company holiday party.

He has also earned four degrees, including an M.A. – Marketing and an M.A. – Human Resources Development from Webster University, as well as a B.A. – Communications and a B.A. – Political Science from the University of Missouri-St. Louis. He's done.

Andy is a proud member of the National Speakers Association (NSA), Florida Speakers Association (FSA), and Association for Applied and Therapeutic Humor (AATH). His website is http://www.andy-masters.com, and he can be contacted at andy@andy-masters.com for speaking availability and volume book discounts for your event or organization. Of course, you can also follow Andy's every move from enduring flight delays to lying in bed eating a bag of Doritos on Facebook or twitter.com/andy_masters.

TABLE OF CONTENTS

1.	There's No Substitute for Experience	1
2.	Never Underestimate the Power of First Impressions	4
3.	Be Creative	8
4.	Little Things Mean a Lot	11
5.	Flattery Will Get You Everywhere	14
6.	It's About Honesty, Trust, and Integrity	17
7.	Have a GREAT Sense of Humor	21
8.	Looks Can Be Deceiving	25
9.	It's a Numbers Game (Just keep asking and you're bound to get lucky at some point)	28
10.	Learn to Face REJECTION!	30
11.	Define Your Target Market	33
12.	Find Fun and Unique Ways to Promote Yourself	36
13.	Utilize the Power of the Internet	40
14.	Capitalize On All Social Media Opportunities	43
15.	Do Some Research on Your Prospect First (Without being considered a STALKER)	46
16.	NETWORKING: It's About Relationship Building, Not Just Contact Building	49
17.	Capitalize on The Power of Referrals and Word-of-Mouth Advertising	52
18.	Be Wary of Who People Set You Up With	55
19.	Caveat Emptor (Let the Buyer Beware)	58
20.	Share Testimonials from Previously Satisfied Customers	62
21.	Don't Seem Too Desperate	65
22.	Be Confident	68
23.	Just Be Yourself	71
24.	Timing Is Everything	74
25.	Location. Location. Location.	77
26.	ALWAYS Be Ready (You Never Know Who, When, or Where)	79

27. Sometimes the Best Opportunities Come
When We Least Expect – – – – – – – – – – – – – – – – – 81
28. Failing to Risk is Risking to Fail (Don't Just Stand There
with Your Hands in Your Pockets) – – – – – – – – – – – – 84
29. You've Got To Love The Thrill of the Hunt – – – – – – – – 87
30. Be Assertive, Not Aggressive – – – – – – – – – – – – – – – 90
31. Meticulous Personal Hygiene...IMPORTANT! – – – – – – 92
32. Follow Up. Follow-Up. Follow Up. – – – – – – – – – – – – 95
33. Don't Become Too Nervous or Stressed-Out – – – – – – – 98
34. Don't Embarrass Yourself – – – – – – – – – – – – – – – – – 101
35. Identify Those Red Flags EARLY – – – – – – – – – – – – – 104
36. Take Them Somewhere Unique and Fun – – – – – – – 107
37. Eliminate Your Competition (By Having No Competition) – 109
38. Learn How to Stand Out in a Crowd – – – – – – – – – 112
39. Get Them to Come to You – – – – – – – – – – – – – – – 115
40. Be a GREAT Listener – – – – – – – – – – – – – – – – – – 118
41. Know How to Interpret Nonverbal Communication – 121
42. Deal With the Frustration of Getting Mixed Signals – – 123
43. Master Persuasive Communication, the Art of
Negotiation, and the Ability to Compromise – – – – – 126
44. Deal With Fear of Commitment – – – – – – – – – – – – 129
45. Identify the Objections, and Overcome the Objections – 132
46. PERSISTENCE: Don't Accept "No" For An Answer (That is,
Until They Get A RESTRAINING ORDER) – – – – – – – – 136
47. Buying Them a Few Drinks Never Hurt – – – – – – – – 138
48. If All Else Fails, BEG! – – – – – – – – – – – – – – – – – – 140
49. Sometimes It's Better to Be Lucky Than Good – – – – – 142
50. Be a GREAT Closer – – – – – – – – – – – – – – – – – – – 145
51. Overcome BUYERS' REMORSE – – – – – – – – – – – – – 148
52. Keep Your Customer Satisfied – – – – – – – – – – – – – 150
53. Don't Take The Other Person For Granted – – – – – – – 151
54. Make the Other Person Feel Special – – – – – – – – – – 154

55. Understand Their Wants and Needs – – – – – – – – – 157
56. Don't Be A Cheapskate – – – – – – – – – – – – – – 160
57. Consider Your Return On Investment – – – – – – – – 163
58. Manage Expectations – – – – – – – – – – – – – – – 166
59. Be Up-Front From The Start! – – – – – – – – – – – – 170
60. Sometimes Good Just Isn't Good Enough
    (*We Must Be Awesome!*) – – – – – – – – – – – – – – 172
61. The Customer is Always Right (*Even When
    They are WRONG!*) – – – – – – – – – – – – – – – – 175
62. Avoid DISSATISFACTION At All Costs – – – – – – – – 178
63. Learn to Apologize and Make Up for Your Mistakes – – 181
64. Are You Listening to the Devil on One Shoulder
    Or the Angel on The Other? – – – – – – – – – – – – 184
65. Get Them to Love You and You Can Get Away With
    (*Almost*) Anything – – – – – – – – – – – – – – – – 187
66. Repeat Business (*Keep 'em Coming Back for More*) – – 190
67. Spend Most of Your Time With Those
    Most Important To You – – – – – – – – – – – – – – 193
68. Know When to Cut Your Losses – – – – – – – – – – 196
69. Create an Amicable Breakup (*NEVER Burn Bridges!*) – 199
70. Conduct a Post-Relationship Evaluation – – – – – – – 203
71. Stay Positive and Bounce Back After Disappointments – – 206
72. Gain Hope From Success Stories of Others – – – – – – 209
73. Undertake Goal Setting, Not Goal Settling – – – – – – 212
74. Focus on Personal Development to Be
    The BEST You Can Be – – – – – – – – – – – – – – 215
75. Celebrate Your Successes
    (*Stop and Smell the Dozen Roses*) – – – – – – – – – 218
76. Have Fun! – 221
77. The Ultimate Goal: Building a Long-Term Relationship – – 223

ACKNOWLEDGMENTS

I'd like to thank my Creative Review Team [CRT], consisting of my six talented, funny, and wise friends from across the country: Mike Anderson, Dave Clark, Scott Ginsberg, Steve Hughes, Jenn Navarro, and Christine Ronken.

I'd also like to thank all of my ex-clients and ex-girlfriends for contributing material from times of despair, embarrassing tales, moments of triumph, and life-changing lessons.

A kiss is a symbol.

A kiss says *"I like you."*
A kiss says *"I appreciate you."*
A kiss says *"You are special to me."*

A kiss makes the other person feel wanted.
A kiss makes the other person feel important.
A kiss makes the other person feel warm and fuzzy inside.

How can we make our customers feel such feelings?
How can we make our loved ones feel such feelings...even more?

Over the past several years, I've investigated the eerie similarities between sales and service, and dating and relationships. Extensive research for the book included reminiscing all of my past relationships, reviewing training manuals, and reading as many back issues of *Cosmopolitan* as I could get my hands on. *(Gentlemen, if you aren't reading that material—you are missing out).*

There are principles from our relationships which can help us in sales and service, and principles from sales and service which can help us in our relationships. In fact, I've identified 77 common principles of success which are critical to all.

Why 77?

Hey, 78 just seemed a bit overboard.

Many chapters are filled with irony, many with humor, and many with heart-felt advice that we can truly stop and learn from.

There is a great irony between the sales process and romantic courtship. There is also a great irony between keeping your customer happy, and keeping your significant other happy.

Get the Customer. *Keep the Customer.*

Get the Girl. *Keep the Girl.*

Sales. *Service.*

Dating. *Relationships.*

We are all familiar with the classic storyline of boy meets girl, boy loses girl, boy gets girl back. But, how can we be even better with maintaining our valued relationships, so we don't have to fight to get them back? In the real world, some never come back.

They ride off into the sunset with our dreaded competition.

"Hasta la vista, baby!"

It's easy for singles to become depressed and frustrated, losing confidence and hope with each disappointment. The same is true for those in sales, which has one of the highest rates of alcoholism, high blood pressure, divorce, and suicide of any occupation.

"Sounds GREAT...where do I sign up?"

Therefore, in both business and in life, we need comic relief—in addition to a tool which can help us break through to happiness and success. We need rays of light which bring us hope. We need creative sparks which bring us adrenaline. We need horror stories which cause us to revisit our own misfortunes, helping us laugh about these crazy things called relationships. Business and personal.

Chapter 1

I believe experience in business and relationships begins with your first sale, and your first kiss, respectively. I remember my first experience in sales. It was in 1st grade.

This small sports store nearby sold colored pencils for 99 cents per pack, each imprinted with the name of an NFL team. Everyone at my school said, *"Wow—where did you get those?"* But I wouldn't tell them. Instead, I had this great idea to sell individual pencils for 25 cents each to classmates who wanted to buy the pencil of their favorite team. I even placed a 25 cent up-charge on the most popular teams such as the Dallas Cowboys, Pittsburgh Steelers, and hometown St. Louis Cardinals *(then an NFL team)*.

Business was booming.

I raked in a profit of $2.25 on my first pack alone—tax free.

Then one day, someone else discovered which sports store sold these pencils, and he started selling them for only 10 cents each. His name was Jimmy.

Twerp. He ruined my monopoly.

I considered asking my friend Guido if he would *"take care of the problem"* for me. You know, like biting the erasers off Jimmy's inventory, or something along those lines. However, the ethical businessperson in me overruled that idea, so I instead proposed:

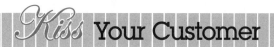

"Hey, Jimmy, if we both sold these pencils at 20 cents each, we would both sell a lot and make a lot of money. We'd both win!"

It was beautiful. At such a young age, I learned a wonderful concept called collaboration. That, and a wonderful concept called *price-fixing*.

Our plan worked great, until someone turned us in to the principal because we wouldn't give him a cut of the action.

Teachers.

Don't they make enough already?

I remember the first girl I ever kissed. I had just graduated 3rd grade. Her name was Debbie Rust. Don't worry, she was much cuter than what her last name implied. Wow, she was cute! I wonder what she looks like today?

Anyway, I vividly remember us play-wrestling around on the ground one day in her backyard, and at just the right moment, just as we caught eyes, I instinctively laid one on her. It was pretty magical. A first kiss is such a special and sentimental milestone in a boy's life. For that finite moment, when my lips touched hers, I was *beaming* inside. I was so *HAPPY!* It was the *HAPPIEST* split-second of my life!!

That's when she punched me in the gut and ran away screaming "MOMMMMM... HELP! ANDY MASTERS JUST KISSED ME!! CALL 9-1-1!!! I'M GONNA DIE!!... AAAAAAAAAAHHHHHHH!!!...I HATE YOU!!!"

That didn't quite encourage me to try that kissing thing again anytime soon.

So, after the emotional scarring wore off a few years later, I began questioning myself. What did I do wrong? What could I do better next time? How can I kiss a girl without having her scream for 9-1-1?

Maybe it was the fact that I hadn't established a strong enough friendship with her yet. Maybe it was the fact that she didn't trust me yet. Or, maybe it was the fact that I was holding a dead frog in my left hand while I kissed her.

The bottom line is, we learn from our experiences in every relationship we have—business and personal. I believe life is a constant cycle of learning, then applying, then learning more, and applying more.

**We are a product of how we apply
the previous experiences in our lives
to our future situations. To apply is to grow.
To ignore is to err.**

Chapter 2

NEVER UNDERESTIMATE THE POWER OF FIRST IMPRESSIONS

Knowing the obvious importance of first impressions in the dating world, I've always enjoyed presenting a small gift for each first date which is related to one of her interests, or perhaps her occupation. Something clever. Something creative. Something for her to remember me by.

So, even if she didn't like me, maybe she'd at least like my gift.

I was running uncharacteristically late for a first date one evening, and suddenly realized I had not bought a present for my date yet. Rats! Fortunately, we were meeting at a restaurant attached to a major mall in St. Louis. She was a die-hard St. Louis Cardinals fan, so I figured I'd run into the sports store to grab a cute Cardinals team item. While I was scurrying down the hall, I saw a familiar face standing by the mall directory on the left.

It was Steve Klein...

...who was a pitcher for the St. Louis Cardinals.

My mind was running faster than my legs:

"What does this mean? What should I do?"

Then, I got it. I ran into the sports store, quickly purchased a $7.99 baseball with a Cardinals logo, and ran back into the hallway with hopes Steve was still there. He was.

I marched directly towards him holding this baseball and a pen, and said, *"Hi, Steve—Sorry to bother you, but I'm five minutes away from a first date with this HUGE Cardinals fan and..."*

Before I could finish, he just smiled and said *"Sure, man... What do you want me to say on it?"*

Fulfilling my request, he swiftly signed:

"Karen -

Good Luck. Andy is one AWESOME guy!

– Steve Klein."

Now, if she only liked me as much as she liked that ball, I might have a 2nd date story to tell about her, too.

But, that's OK. I understand. I wish her the best. Maybe we just weren't a good fit. Sometimes two people just don't have chemistry. I don't take it personally. Blah-blah-blah.

However...

Karen was so impressed with me that she actually put me in contact with one of her single friends, telling her how nice, clever, and creative I was. That's right, a REFERRAL! *(Seriously, how often does THAT happen in the dating world?)*

Lesson learned: In either business or dating, even if a person isn't a good match for you or your product, they might know someone who is.

I again realized we can create a dramatic impact with first impressions—with such little cost and such little time. There are so many easy, quick, and inexpensive ways to be clever and creative in this world. So... WHY DON'T PEOPLE DO IT MORE OFTEN?

Seriously, what's our excuse?

"I'm not that creative."

Sure you are.

"I don't have time to be that creative."

Really? You don't have time to impact the most important people in your life and career?

Perhaps the ultimate first impression would be considered *"Love at first sight."* It's impossible to create a better first impression than that, right? Maybe this should be our goal.

So, is it possible to achieve love at first sight in the business world? What about the first time you laid eyes on a product—when you had the feeling right away that THIS ONE was for you?

"We can stop shopping now. THIS IS IT. This is EXACTLY what I've been looking for. LET'S GO!!"

I know. It happens to me all the time at Victoria's Secret, too.

Have you ever had that same feeling about someone in sales, or anyone who could provide a service for you? Perhaps it was a financial representative, a real estate agent, or even a dentist. You probably have.

If so, why?

What characteristics were you looking for that they possessed?

What was their first 60 seconds of conversation?

How was their appearance?

Did they have a fungus-like substance hanging from their teeth?

If they handed you something, was it unique, or was it boring?

Please, no more bland business cards. No more squirt bottles. No more thermal mugs with your company logo. Despite what you might believe, people don't want to see *"Ed's Manure Hauling"* every morning when they drink their coffee. What would make the other person feel like your gift was just for *them*? What would make the other person go *"Wow!"* What autograph would they want on that baseball?

We're all experienced enough to understand that first impressions include a great smile, eye contact, and a firm handshake. That's *"Life Lessons 101."* Take that to the next level by having FUN in life and being creative with every first impression. You'll be surprised how much you will look forward to that next meeting when you have a *"Wow"* moment waiting for someone.

By the way, these principles don't just apply to a first impression, but also a last impression—which is the impression someone was left with the last time that person saw you.

We should always try to create lasting last impressions with everyone we come in contact with throughout the day, new contact or old.

7

I once took this first date out to a really nice restaurant (*I believe it was Hooters or something*). My gift purchase was a bit of a challenge, since she wasn't currently working and I didn't know much about her. However, I did know this date was actually into... bass fishing. This was GREAT, because I'm also into bass fishing.

I had just the right surprise in mind.

So, just after our food was delivered, and just when the mood was right, I reached into my pocket and handed across to her a... PURPLE PLASTIC WORM.

Now, I knew this was a little risky depending on her sense of humor, so I figured I would get one of two responses. Either:

"OH MY GOSH... That is SO funny and creative!
No one has EVER given me a worm on a first date before!"

OR

"Get away from me, you FREAK."

I'm happy to report that she fell for the gag hook, line, and sinker (*pun intended*).

Talk about a lasting first impression. That's right. **I'm confident that still to this day, when she sees a worm, she thinks of me.**

That's powerful stuff.

You can't buy that kind of staying power.

By the way, gentlemen, if you plan on trying this, but you get the feeling it's not going to work, just play it safe and keep your worm in your pocket.

I've always taken pride in being a clever and thoughtful gift giver, whether it was for a holiday, a birthday, or—most importantly—as a surprise. On one occasion, I had a dozen roses delivered to the workplace of my girlfriend the day *before* Valentine's Day. The card read:

"If you received these tomorrow, it wouldn't be a surprise. Besides, you deserve your roses before any other woman in America."

Gentlemen, please try this, and brace yourself for the bursting-of-affection that will ensue. Go ahead and send the *"Thank You"* email to: andy@andy-masters.com.

There are several companies who produce customized chocolate gift items that include edible logos, edible photos, and up to 60 characters of edible text *(so, yes, you can literally eat your words)*.

Awesome stuff!

I actually met the owner of one of these chocolate logo companies, persuaded him that he was under-charging for these products, and convinced him there was a monster opportunity selling his products in bulk to corporations for their clients. I hope he took my advice *(well, maybe not about raising the price)*.

One holiday season, I uploaded pictures of myself with a Santa hat that included clever, personalized holiday greetings for recipients, such as *"Please don't bite my head off!"* I've given these to family, friends, and favorite clients at the end of the year. I've had several people tell me they didn't eat it, but rather saved it in their freezer to show all of their friends.

All for only $6.99 each.

Still sending boring bulk holiday cards? Come on! Here is your annual opportunity to wipe out your competition and flash that humor and creativity. Just Google "chocolate logo," and you'll have several such companies to choose from.

And, in case you're paranoid about chocolate gifts melting into a mud pie by delivery, try these websites for non-edible creative items with a similar personalized concept:

www.personalizationmall.com

www.agiftpersonalized.com

www.vistaprint.com

There was an ad agency rep from Chicago who had been trying desperately to get business with a top prospect. In a final attempt, she sent one baby booty in a tube along with a note which read: *"Now that I have one foot in the door, I'd love to get the other one in, too."*

Cheesy? Yes.

Did it work? Yes.

You know, I've often wondered something about that example: When she followed-up the next day to be sure the package arrived OK, would that be considered making a *"Booty call"*?

I couldn't resist.

Creativity also means doing the *unexpected* in life, with all of our relationships. People love surprises, so surprise them. Show up unexpectedly at their work with a gift. Sneak up behind them in the hallway and say *"BOO!"* Be waiting for them naked when they open up the shower curtain. (*Warning:* Only try this last one if your client has a REALLY good sense of humor.)

Chapter 4

There is a principle I must share from my program titled **From Time Management to Work-Life SUPERHERO!** It's a concept I developed called **"15 MINUTES OR LESS/15 DOLLARS OR LESS."** This principle illustrates that each of us can make an amazing impact on someone's life today, using just 15 minutes or less of our time, and 15 dollars or less of our money.

I once presented at an event hosted by one of the University of Michigan campuses, and enjoyed dinner with my client after the program. During casual conversation while deciding what to order, Marilyn mentioned she "goes hog-wild" for A&W Root Beer.

Good thing she didn't say Dom Perignon, since dinner was on me.

I made a mental note of her affinity for A&W Root Beer, and pondered a few alternatives on my flight back. When I arrived home, I jumped online for less than 15 minutes and ordered a case of A&W Root Beer for less than $15.00, which was delivered to Marilyn's home address within three days.

Pretty cool.

The moral of the story?

I was re-booked there the following year, right?

Ehhhhh… no.

I was referred to a colleague who booked me the following year, right?

Ehhhhh… no.

In fact, over three years went by, and I didn't hear anything from Marilyn.

Sad. But I was used to that from women.

Until one day, I received a phone call.

Marilyn: "Andy... Hi—It's Marilyn from up in Michigan, do you remember me?"

Andy: "Sure I remember you, Marilyn. How are you doing?"

Marilyn: "I'm great! Hey, I wanted to tell you that I'm so sorry I haven't kept in touch. You're not going to believe this, but, less than two weeks after you presented up here... well, I quit my job! I'm doing something completely different now. But, guess what...?"

Andy: "What?"

Marilyn: "I just became chair of the planning committee for our upcoming conference, and we'd love for you to be our keynote speaker. Are you available on August 23rd?"

Andy: "Yes... that sounds great. Would love to do it!"

After that program I presented on August 23rd, Marilyn and I again enjoyed dinner together. I asked her a question.

Andy: "So, Marilyn, I have to ask...After three years, what made you decide to track me down to present this program for you?"

Marilyn: "Sure, Andy. I've been waiting three years to tell you this. You know, I love your program. You're really a great speaker. But, there are plenty of other great speakers out there who also present great programs. Do you remember that case of A&W Root Beer you shipped to my home?"

Andy: "Sure... absolutely."

Marilyn: "Andy, do you know I STILL have one can of that A&W Root Beer in my refrigerator, that I show my friends and family when they come over? That was the greatest small gesture that anyone has ever done for me when it wasn't my birthday or Christmas."

Wow.

As great as we think we are at what we do, there is another person, or another company, who can probably perform the same function or service just as well as we can.

So, what makes the difference?

The little things. The little things which take 15 minutes or less, and 15 dollars or less. What an amazing investment of so little time, and so little money.

The excuses we subconsciously tell ourselves are *"I don't have enough time"* and *"I don't have enough money."*

Sure we do. We should *always* have 15 minutes or less, and 15 dollars or less, to spend on the most important people in our life and career.

Fifteen minutes per day is just 1/100th of our time.

I once shared this story during my program for a chapter of Meeting Professionals International (MPI) in Richmond, Virginia. During casual conversation at lunch, I mentioned to one of the event organizers that Fanta Orange was my favorite drink. Three days after my program, I had a box waiting for me outside my front door. It was a collectable Fanta Orange glass purchased from Coca-Cola.com.

I had a smile on my face from ear to ear.

This totally made my day.

Then I thought to myself, "I have to include this in my program!" So, I visited Coca-Cola.com to download a photo of the glass, and discovered this product was just $4.97—on clearance for $1.97!

AWESOME!!

So, what amazing impact can you make today with your special client, significant other, employee, or new contact, using just 15 minutes or less and 15 dollars or less?

Chapter 5

FLATTERY WILL GET YOU EVERYWHERE

According to the book *Are You Normal About Sex, Love, and Relationships?*, 51 percent of people use flattery to initially show interest with another person, while 23 percent still utilize the schoolyard approach of sending word out through a friend.

These people are also referred to as CHICKENS.

I think we all know what fast-growing segment of the population make up this shameful 23 percent.

Seniors.

Haven't retirement communities heard of online dating yet?

> **Friend:** *Hey, Edgar... Ethel thinks you're cute."*
>
> **Edgar:** *"Ethel plays the FLUTE?"*
>
> **Friend:** *No, Edgar... she thinks you're CUTE."*

When using a 3rd party, sometimes the message can get lost in translation.

Besides being direct, a major key with using flattery is to be sure it is original and sincere, not just a blatant attempt to *"kiss their butt."* This can be a real turn-off and is easily detectable in most situations.

Admittedly, I once stole a line from a top role model of mine in the areas life, leadership, and love: Dr. Evil of the *Austin Powers* trilogy. In the movie *Austin Powers 2: The Spy Who Shagged Me*, Dr. Evil was chit-chatting with a female love interest at the breakfast buffet and said, *"Try the Hot Pockets. They're breath-taking."* I always thought that was funny, and wanted to use it on my own someday.

So, right after appetizers were delivered on a hopeful first date, I leaned across the table and said *"Try the chicken fingers. They're breathtaking."*

Of course, that line garnered one of those "Is he serious" looks I've come to know quite well. However, later in the evening, when the moonlight struck her eyes, I said to her softly in a romancing voice *"You are even more breathtaking than the chicken fingers."*

Original flattery.

Creative flattery.

Yep, I pretty much had her from that moment on.

In business, we must be sure our flattery doesn't cross the line. It's been increasingly recommended over the last 20 years to avoid complimenting people on their attire or their looks. In our present world of political correctness and sexual harassment lawsuits, there is a chance your compliment might be misinter-preted *(I still haven't figured out how "I think you're HOT" can be misinterpreted)* or make the other person feel uncomfortable *(Ladies, feel free to make me feel uncomfortable anytime).*

Focus on finding better sources for your compliments, in business and in life. One should always strive for "legitimate" flattery, as opposed to "token" flattery. What is something you truly admire about the business, background, or accomplishments of the other person? Perhaps make a keen or insightful observation.

"I noticed you had an article published in Entrepreneur *last month. GREAT stuff! It was so creative, I made copies for everyone in the office and advised them to share with our clients, as well."*

This will truly impress the other person, and will show you were conscientious enough to acknowledge something different. People are bored by token compliments such as *"nice tie,"* *"nice car,"* or *"you sure have a great company."* That's as original as talking about the weather.

So, what do you like to be complimented on or recognized for? What do you really hope people notice or appreciate about you? I bet it's not that you wear nice ties or a nice dress.

Flattery is a reflection of the person giving the compliment. Are you shallow and boring, or intelligent and clever? Next time, try using words like:

Colorful.

Dazzling.

Inspirational.

Breathtaking.

Chapter 6

It's About HONESTY, TRUST and INTEGRITY

Below is an old joke about the public perception of salesperson honesty:

Question: *"How do you know a salesperson is lying?"*

Answer: *"Their lips are moving."*

Below are survey results from TopDatingTips.com, where the question was posed:

"On a date, do you believe your companion is 100% truthful?"

Yes – 22%   No – 78%

Indeed, I thought about creating a great invention called the *"Pinnochio Portable Lie Detector"* we could carry around to test people with, but I bet lawyers and politicians would ban it. Although, maybe it'll become an iPHONE application soon. That would be GREAT!

"Place your finger on the iPHONE HERE while answering each question. If you answer honestly, the ringtone "Honesty" by Billy Joel will play. If you answer dishonestly, the phone will vibrate immediately and you will be shocked by a 125-volt charge."

Hmmm…

Just imagine the possibilities:

"Did you cheat at golf? Did you cheat on me? Did you cheat on your taxes? Did you lie on your résumé? Have you been drinking? Are you SURE this used car has never been in an accident before? Are you SURE you spent the night at Tommy's house, young man?"

In fact, this would really come in handy in education, assisting 1st grade teachers to maintain honesty in the classroom.

TEACHER: *"Johnny, did you cheat on your homework?"*
JOHNNY: *"Ummmm... No."*
iPHONE: *"ZZZAAAPPP!!!"*
TEACHER: *"Now, go to the nurse's office and don't ever lie to me again!"*

The bottom line is, people are cynical. This is a critical hurdle to overcome. **Earning someone's trust in either business or dating takes time, and the development of a relationship.** The other person won't trust you unless you give them a reason to trust you. It also takes a long time to regain trust after you've lost it.

I learned that lesson at a young age.

You know those silly games little kids play?

When I was 4 years old, my friends and I played this game in my backyard called *"Close your eyes and I'll put something in your mouth."*

It was a lot of fun. We played every day after I got home from Kinder Care.

We started with the simple stuff. Dirt. Blades of grass. Maybe a bug or two.

Then one day, I raised the ante on my friend Suzie, when I slid a slimy 6-inch worm into her mouth.

She swallowed the whole thing.

Yikes.

I knew I was going to be in BIG trouble as she ran home screaming to her Dad: *"AAAAHHHHH... IT WAS SLIMY, IT WAS SLIMY!!! ANDY MADE ME DO IT!!!"*

Even at such a young age, I did what any stand-up guy would do. I hid under my bed crying until my Mom stormed in.

"Mommy, NO!! Not the iPHONE again!!"

OK, fortunately for me, no iPHONEs were around quite yet.

Nevertheless, Suzie and I didn't play with each other for the next six weeks. Then one day, there was a knock on my front door. It was Suzie. She said she wanted to play that game again. I shook my head and said *"No."* She said *"Yes."* I said *"No."* She said *"Yes."* I said *"OK."*

So, we went over to her driveway, and she said *"This time it's your turn, Andy. So, close your eyes and I'll put something in your mouth."*

"Just trust me," she said, as she handed me some type of jug. *"But you have to drink the WHOLE THING."*

She must have read the *"I'm gullible"* sign on my forehead, because I actually said *"OK."*

So, I drank the whole thing, projectile vomited, and was rushed to the hospital to have my stomach pumped.

It was battery acid from her brothers' go-cart.

True story. Paybacks are a… well…

Yep, it took me 25 years to regain my trust in women after that *(or at least the ability to close my eyes and open my mouth for them—which made kissing VERY awkward.)*

Statistically speaking, I am TRULY one of the very few males who have NEVER cheated on any girl in the history of his life, even going back to 8th grade. I'm very proud of this fact.

Of course, it wasn't for lack of trying.

It's been hard enough to find ONE woman willing to go out with me at a time. Let's face it, Tiger Woods I am *not*.

The business world also provides us opportunities for honesty lessons in the strangest of ways.

Once I was presenting a small workshop for about 75 marketing professionals in Orlando, Florida. At the end of the program, one of the audience members in the front row stood up to leave, and dropped a $100 bill on the floor behind him. No one else saw this, but I indeed said, *"Sir, I think you just dropped that $100 bill on the floor."*

You know, this gentleman has since referred me to many of his colleagues who plan trainings and events, and not just because he enjoyed my program. I feel like I have a friend for life.

It doesn't matter if it's a $100 bill, a $5 bill, or nickel. Integrity is a character trait.

There's an old saying that *"integrity is doing the right thing when nobody is looking."*

Or, when someone has their eyes closed and you're putting something in their mouth.

Chapter 7

HAVE A GREAT SENSE of HUMOR

A survey of 1,000 women by Harlequin Publishing found the most important trait in a mate was sense of humor, even more important than good looks and physique.

Thank God.

Take that, Gold's Gym muscleheads! *(Sorry, I didn't mean that. Really.)*

People will enjoy speaking with you on the phone if you have a great phone personality. People are more willing to go to lunch with you if you are entertaining company, rather than hearing you talk about your product or service the entire time as they count the minutes until the check comes.

People will want to date you, hire you, and buy from you if they like you.

Scientifically, laughter actually helps the human body create endorphins, which relieve pain and induce euphoria. Both of which are handy in business and relationships.

Therefore, I believe everyone should make a *focused attempt* at incorporating more humor in the workplace, and in their lives outside of the workplace.

If you are a manager, get in the habit of sending a related business cartoon to your team every Monday morning. It's a nice morale boost to start the week. **Employees have enough pressure. They need to laugh.**

Besides weekly cartoons, you can easily find funny articles, blogs, pictures or videos by searching Google, Google Images, or YouTube. Use the Google Alerts tool to notify you each day for new material on phrases such as "business humor," "funny dating," or "financial jokes," etc. If you saw something hysterical on Jay Leno's "Headlines" segment that related to your industry, but you didn't have your TIVO running, simply visit www.nbc.com the next day to share the same clip with others.

Find jokes that work, and stick with them.

Since my childhood, I've been pretty good about cleaning my plate, not leaving any food to spare. However, I love leaving just half of a burnt French fry on my plate at a restaurant now, then joking to the server *"Can you wrap that up for me?"*

It gets a laugh every time. Either that or an eye-roll.

Similarly, since I'm not a fan of whipped cream, I always push it to the side of the dessert plate, asking the waitress for a take-home box with a wink: *"We're saving that for later ;)"*

I'd suggest using that one with a date rather than a client.

Lastly, I always carry several denominations of children's play currency in my wallet, which are sold in the toy aisle of any department store. These bills are actually quite realistic. They are just bleach white and much smaller than standard bills, such as the size of monopoly money. I love having fun by confidently slapping a few big bills down on the table when the check comes, and saying straight-faced lines to the waiter such as:

> *"Alright everybody, dinner is on me!"*
> *"Do you have change for a $100?"*
> *"There's more where THAT came from."*
> *"Sorry, I must have left it in the laundry."*
> *"What, are you saying my money's not good here, pal?"*

It's pretty funny.
I guess you just have to be there.

Now I'm going to give away one of my best dating secrets ever *(which also comes in handy when entertaining clients)*. It's called my *"Funny Story Cheat Sheet."* Yep, every first date I ever went on, I carried a small piece of paper in my back right pocket. It included several of my funniest jokes and stories, along with other juicy conversation starters.

It worked great, until one evening on a goodnight kiss, a girl reached behind me and put her hand inside that back pocket!

"Hey, what is this?"

"Oh, nothing. I'm actually writing a funny book on ridiculous dating stories and am always compiling material. So, tell me again about your phobia of Jack-O-Lanterns...?"

As a professional speaker, I learned early in my career **"Make them laugh or you're DEAD."** People will pay more attention, learn more, will like you more, and will purchase more from you if they laugh.

On that note, be sure to test your humor out first. Nothing is worse than launching an iffy joke in front of an important audience and it bombs. Trust me, I've tried it.

Zig Ziglar, one of the most brilliant motivational speakers in history, knew the power of incorporating humor in his presentations. Throughout his career, Zig would strategically place some type of wit, joke, or funny example every seven minutes during his presentation, no matter the audience or topic. As he determined through research, attention span begins to dip as time between jokes lingered. People pay attention because they don't want to miss the next joke!

"What if the nature of my job or presentation is serious?"

This means it is ESPECIALLY important for you to include humor. Trust me, if you work in finance or insurance, people are dreading hearing from you, even if it's just a 5-minute overview during the weekly staff meeting.

Southwest Airlines has long made a name for itself not only with low fares, but also with funny commercials and colorful

flight attendants. And, what could be more serious than safety instructions for those about ready to take off? I recall one flight attendant who described the restrooms as their *"spacious and luxurious powder rooms,"* and final instructions included the comment *"this is a long flight, so if you're traveling with children this evening... we're sorry."*

Even funeral home directors like to laugh. Goodness, they need humor in their lives more than any of us, don't they? If you are ever presenting for this group, add something like: *"Fortunately for your business, the death rate is still hovering at about 100%."*

You'll knock 'em dead.

Chapter 8

LOOKS CAN BE DECEIVING

Some things in this world aren't always as they appear. Just ask this guy:

Man: *"So, hot stuff, what do you do for a living?"*

Woman: *"I'm a female impersonator."*

One evening, I arrived early to a small sales program I was presenting which was hosted at a quaint bar/restaurant in North Miami Beach. The outside of the venue looked normal, but when I looked around inside, I noticed the décor was quite peculiar.... even strangely risqué. I was greeted by a tall, provocatively dressed "hostess" whose Adam's apple was bigger than mine. Then I looked at the rest of the clientele and employees and it dawned on me:

My program was being hosted at a TRANSVESTITE CLUB.

This minor detail was unannounced to me, or my audience, prior to the event. Supposedly, the event organizer didn't know this fact either, but wanted to *"branch out and try a different meeting place this time."* Yeah, transvestite clubs are always GREAT training venues for conservative professionals over the age of 50 who want to hear about networking and referrals. Thanks a lot.

While we were busy placing wagers on the original gender of each staff member, the emcee for the evening—also an employee—took the stage to introduce me. I believe his/her name for the evening was "Cher."

He/She said: *"We all need to listen to this program tonight because, as you know, everybody is in sales. Hell, I try to sell myself over on Lincoln and 149th Street every night."*

I swear, I can't make this stuff up.

Fortunately, I present my programs in much more reputable establishments now. I've moved up to brothels.

Nevertheless, looks can be deceiving, and in the sales world we need to be careful not to stereotype. Salespeople are always eager to scope out a potential customer and make immediate judgments based on looks. This can be a dangerous trap to fall into.

Even if someone isn't capable of buying your product now, *they might be capable in the future.* **Even if someone doesn't need your product now,** *they might know someone who does.* **People know when they are being pre-judged, and they don't like it.**

I remember when I was pre-judged as a consumer.

I was a broke college student visiting Las Vegas on a school-sponsored trip, and stopped into the very expensive Gucci store at Caesar's Palace. The humorless sales attendant must have identified my not-so-upscale presence as I entered. It must have been my Guns 'N Roses T-shirt and McDonaldland cookie bag that gave it away.

She inquired *"Are you looking for something in particular, sir?"*

I said *"Yeah, the mannequin in the front window is pretty hot. Is she for sale?"*

No response.

I said *"Actually, I'm looking for the least expensive thing in here, so I can say I bought my girlfriend something from the Gucci store in Las Vegas. Do you have a keychain or anything?"*

"Sir," she said in a condescending tone. *"This store is intended for serious patrons who are in the market for the finest Gucci products in the world."*

"Oh," I responded. "Well, I'm in the market for the finest Gucci product in the world sold for less than ten dollars. Preferably something I can put on layaway."

Not amused, she said "Sir...if you must, the least expensive items we carry are the handkerchiefs on the front display table. They are $47.50 each."

I said "$47.50 EACH? For something that catches SNOT??"

"TAX NOT INCLUDED!" Ms. Snooty added.

I paused, then replied "Oh, yeah...well I'll have you know I just hit it big on the nickel slots, so I'll take TWO of them. One for my girlfriend, and ONE FOR THE NEXT TIME I RUN OUT OF TOILET PAPER. What do you think about THAT?"

She said "FINE."

I said "FINE."

So, I took my $95 worth of handkerchiefs and left.

Of course, now that I can actually afford to buy something from there, trust me, I DON'T.

I buy all my stuff from TJ Maxx instead just to spite her.

That'll teach her.

Chapter 9

IT'S A NUMBERS GAME

(JUST KEEP ASKING AND YOU'RE BOUND TO GET LUCKY AT SOME POINT)

By far the biggest mistake I made early in my dating life, besides talking with my mouth full, was that I didn't take nearly enough risks approaching women. Some of my friends were just the opposite. They would hit on *anything*, no matter where we were. Waitresses. Flight Attendants. Mannequins. You name it.

Hey, at least a mannequin can't say *"Get away from me, you FREAK."*

I had one friend named Alex who would get shot down a LOT at singles bars, and the rest of us would get a big laugh out of watching him. It was GREAT! He was funny entertainment for us cool guys who stood a safe distance from the crossfire of the meat-market battleground. We were smart.

In fact, we were so smart that we left with as many phone numbers as when we entered the place five hours earlier.... NONE. That's because we stood in the corner talking about sports the entire time while buying expensive drinks for each other trying to look cool. But, hey—at least we left with our dignity, and our self-confidence was still in tact.

Soon, I began to realize that Alex was getting plenty more action than we were. He would actually go out on dates. A LOT of them. And, some of these women were beautiful, intelligent, and successful, too. But, wait a second—that doesn't make any sense. Alex is a total DORK. He's 31 years old, works at Pizza Hut, and lives in his parents' basement! What were they thinking? Don't they know what they're missing? Why aren't they going out with someone like ME?!?!

So, I quickly learned that Alex's trick was having no fear of rejection, and to just keep asking. If you ask 1,2,3,4,5,6,7,8,9,10... 15... 20 women out, you're bound to get lucky at some point. The more you stick your neck out, the more success you'll have. The less you stick your neck out, the less success you'll have.

One of the first things I learned as a sales manager was the philosophy that *"Sales is Math."* The more prospects my sales-people would engage, the more appointments they would set. The more appointments they would set, the more they would subsequently sell...even if they weren't that great.

What's interesting is, the more prospects they would engage, the more their success percentage would ultimately increase. Why? First, they steadily became better at engaging prospects through *"practice makes perfect."* Second, they steadily became numb to rejection, so the fear of asking bothered them less. Third, since they eventually closed more sales, their confidence increased, which increased the level of comfort they had to approach their next prospect. This created a domino effect, and in turn, a great cycle of success.

The more comfortable and confident you are to approach people, the more people you will approach, and the more success you'll have.

Just as in dating.

Chapter 10

A piece of rejection advice for women: Men appreciate any rejection method in which you let us down easy, even if it's not the truth. That's right, honesty is *NOT* the best policy. We have egos to protect, so, please...LIE! LIE! LIE!

Often, it's not necessarily the number of rejections, but the method of rejection which hurts. Some sting more than others. In either sales or dating, there are those who practice the "LET-YOU-DOWN-EASY" method of rejection, vs. the "PUNCH-YOU-IN-THE-GUT" method of rejection. For example:

The Dating LET-YOU-DOWN-EASY method of rejection:

"Oh, I'm sorry...Thanks so much for the offer. You seem like a really nice guy, but I'm already in a relationship."

The Dating PUNCH-YOU-IN-THE-GUT method of rejection:

"Sorry, but I'm allergic to DORKS."

The Sales LET-YOU-DOWN-EASY method of rejection:

"We really enjoyed meeting with you and were very impressed with your services, but unfortunately the folks upstairs have tightened up the budget a bit too much this year. Best of luck to you."

The Sales PUNCH-YOU-IN-THE-GUT method of rejection:

"If you come within 50 feet of our front door again, we're calling security."

Importantly, there are some common rejections acceptable in the business world which aren't necessarily appropriate in the dating world, such as:

"Sorry, but I've decided to go with someone less expensive."

"Sorry, but I found someone else who is more responsive to my needs."

"Sorry, but this was probably just a temporary thing as I work my way up."

Ultimately, how you respond to adversity in life (such as rejection) defines your character, and your long-term success. As with anything, you can respond positively or negatively to a rejection. Don't be childish, and say something along the lines of:

"Yeah, well I didn't like you, anyway. You look like Bozo the clown, on a bad hair day!"

That could be dangerous. He might be in charge of vendor selection again next year.

Always try to place a positive spin on business rejections, using a response such as:

"I completely understand, and thank you for your consideration. By the way, do you have any colleagues who might also be looking for similar services?"

Maybe your prospect feels guilty enough about not giving you any business that they will actually try to help you out.

Or, you can always try to help a fellow salesperson who could provide a completely different product or service:

"By the way, I noticed you will be filming a portion of your event. I have a friend who is one of the best videographers in the business. Is it OK if I have her call you or send over some samples?"

As will be covered in networking and referrals, **if you set up a salesperson or business with a big account, you've got a friend for life.**

Most people provide excuses of why they aren't interested in us or our products. But, excuses aren't reasons. They just cushion the truth. In the educational 2005 film *Hitch*, Will Smith's character Alex "Hitch" Hitchens explained that when a woman says:

"'I'm really into my career right now,'...what she's really saying is 'Get away from me now.'"

So true.

People only make excuses for things they really don't want.

If what you have to offer is AWESOME enough, people will find the time (and money) for it.

The 2004 book, and subsequent 2009 film, *He's Just Not That Into You*, highlighted the concept *"don't take things personally."* While this echoes a comforting phrase your mom or manager would tell you after a series of critical rejections, we all must take it to heart. We might have a great product... for the wrong person. Or, we might have a great product for the right person, but at the wrong time.

Rejections are part of the game, and that which we survive makes us stronger. The more rejections we receive simply make us appreciate the triumphs we earn even more.

And, for all single guys who are also in sales... GOD BLESS YOU. That's a lot of rejections flying around in your lives.

Chapter 11

DEFINE
YOUR TARGET MARKET

In either sales or in dating, sometimes we're tempted to just take anything that comes our way.

> "So, what's your type?"
> "Anyone who will say 'YES.'"

I had one friend who responded to that question by answering "*single and breathing*." Hopefully, your standards in both business and life are a bit higher than that.

However, too many people "stumble" into their careers, their customers, or their relationships. I believe in every aspect of life, you should *get picky!* Target exactly what you want, then develop a plan of attack to go get it. This is your life. Don't settle for anything less than exactly what you want, in business or relationships.

Let's say there are 100 men in a bar. One of the men asks a woman out on a date, and she says "Yes." Is the woman saying "Yes" because she has identified that this individual is her best potential match vs. the other 99 men, or simply because he is the only one who happened to ask her out? If the latter, then the guy is choosing her—she's not choosing the guy.

Don't be a victim of happenstance in life. Understand what your ideal match is, then use all available strategic means to meet your match. Try this exercise on a sheet of paper:

In Dating: *"Who is your ideal match?"*
What are their characteristics?
Smart, funny, tan, blonde? *(Sorry, Ladies—I'm already taken.)*
What are their morals and values?
What lifestyle do they want to live?
What political and religious views do they have?
What are they looking for in a partner?
(Does it match what you have to offer?)

In Business: *"Who is your ideal customer?"*
What are their characteristics?
Upscale, younger, active, urban, *infinite budgets?*
What type of positions do they hold?
What associations are they a member of?
What blogs do they chatter on?
What are they looking for in a supplier?
(Does it match what you provide?)

If you were your ideal match, where would you hang out?
If you were your ideal customer, where would you hang out?

So, where are you hanging out?

Always put yourself in environments which breed success, where your target market is. You will lessen your amount of rejections in life when you ask the right people.

The closest female friend I've ever had, Christine, became tired of "falling into" a series of haphazard relationships. Once she actually dated someone whose last name was "Dumm." Like THAT wasn't a dead giveaway. Ultimately, she created a "Top

10 Requirements" list of her ideal man, and posted this list on her refrigerator. Qualifications included *"He must like reading,"* *"He must be career-oriented,"* and *"He must love the outdoors."* Amazingly, number 10 on her list was none other than: *"He must like Andy Masters."*

Ha... Talk about picky! Well, some challenges are more difficult than others, I suppose.

Christine then made sure the environments she put herself in were congruent with the type of guy she was looking for. No more hanging out at monster truck rallies for her. Christine finally met her career-oriented *"Mr. Right"* on a company sponsored float trip. They are happily married today, and enjoy evenings reading in bed together.

> *"If you don't know where you are going,*
> *any road will get you there."*
> *– Lewis Carroll*

In business and in life, you must first define what you are looking for. If what you find fits what you are looking for, it's legit. If it doesn't fit, you must acquit.

FIND FUN and UNIQUE WAYS TO PROMOTE YOURSELF

Times sure have changed. People have discovered new ways to market themselves everywhere. I now find website addresses scripted into bathroom stalls instead of sleazy phone numbers.

Thumbs up for creative, low-cost advertising in front of a captive audience, I suppose.

In either business or dating, once a target market is identified, we must then identify the best methods of marketing to our target market:

Advertising? Events and promotions? Internet/Email?
Telemarketing? Door-to-Door? Skywriting? Sidewalk Chalk?

Predictably, I've always been a fan of funny and unique ways that companies and people have promoted themselves. One example of such humor and creativity is this billboard, which can be seen alongside warm climate highways across the U.S.:

"Your Wife Is HOT!"

(followed below with):

"You'd better get your AC fixed."

A creative CEO of a mundane concrete repair franchise, "The Crack Team," hit the jackpot with this award winning slogan:

"A dry crack is a happy crack!"

Beyond just cracking people up, "The Crack Team" revenues have grown exponentially over the past 10 years.

"The Crack Team" now sells T-shirts and hats on its website *www.mrhappycrack.com*, and has been featured on *CNN*, *The Wall Street Journal*, and *Advertising Age* magazine.

I suppose that slogan worked a bit better than the alternative, *"Just say YES to crack!"*

Finally, an Australian beauty salon came up with this upfront company name to entice potential patrons wanting to boost their appearance:

"Yesterday I Was Ugly!"

No word on how many clients ask for refunds if they are still ugly AFTER their appointments.

Fun concepts can also include promoting yourself for a new job, in addition to sending just a résumé. A good friend of mine, Steve, created a promotional flyer displaying two pictures of himself, along with headlines which read: *"Hire One Steve, Get One Free."* It included the phrases *"Twice the creativity—Twice the productivity—Twice the enthusiasm,"* and was complete with his phone number imprinted within the barcode.

While impressed, I'm sure the hiring company didn't give him twice the vacation time. But he was hired, nonetheless.

Of course, with all of these great concepts that work in business and career, I thought to myself one day:

"Wouldn't it be great if...?"

Wouldn't it be great if we could utilize such clever and unique promotions in the dating world?

So, after my first book was released, I decided to create this great promotion:

"Go on a first date with Andy, get a FREE autographed copy of his book! No obligation!!"

This works GREAT with hot librarians, by the way.

All two of them.

Recently, I ran into a good friend and his new girlfriend, Mandy, at an event in St. Louis. I knew she looked familiar from years before, but I just couldn't place her. So, when a group of us began reminiscing about past dating misfortunes, we shared this exchange:

> **MANDY:** *"Yeah, some guy gave me an autographed copy of his book on a first date once. I sold it in e-Bay the next day for $1.50."*
>
> **ANDY:** *"Yeah... ummm... that was me."*
>
> **MANDY:** *"Oh."*
>
> **ANDY:** *"Can I at least get 75 cents back?"*

Glad to see THAT made a lasting impression.

Lesson learned: Even clever promotions won't work if the customer doesn't like the product.

It's good to know I wasn't alone applying such marketing techniques to the dating world, such as the creative Utah bachelor who posted this HUGE highway billboard:

"Hi, I'm Lance! Let's Go Out!"

This billboard was complete with his photo and website www.datelance.com, while listing five features:

- ♥ *Returned Missionary*
- ♥ *Ex-BYU Basketball Player*
- ♥ *Harvard MBA*
- ♥ *Loves Kids*
- ♥ *Sense of Humor*

No word on how many accidents he caused with single female passers-by.

Predictably, Lance is actually a marketing professional. Not predictably, though, Lance is still actively searching after several years *(maybe he's only found two Utah wives so far).*

Lastly, if you think a woman would never do something like this, think again. An Australian woman posted a highway billboard with this simple headline in extremely large letters: "HUSBAND WANTED," along with her contact info.

Now that's direct *(and to the point)* marketing.

Chapter 13

UTILIZE THE POWER OF THE INTERNET

If one needs help identifying prospects within their target market, there are direct marketing lists anyone can buy, view, or download online, for almost any individual demographic. This includes lists of people living in optimal zip codes, ages 30-40, divorced within the last five years, even with certain income levels.

These are GREAT for relationship seekers. Comes in handy for business purposes, too, I suppose.

You can even segment a population by bra size if you want.

Ok, maybe not.

But someday.

Nevertheless, the Internet is a powerful tool to help us zero-in on individuals within our target market, and is a great time-saver. It sure beats the old days of aimless cold-calling I remember...

Flipping relentlessly through the phone book. Making call after call after call. Getting rejection after rejection, sometimes even before I finished my greeting:

"Hello, my name is Andy—" CLICK!

Fortunately, those days are over. I graduated to ONLINE DATING to find my women.

That's right... no more smoky bars. No more cover charges. No more in-person rejections and painful face-slappings.

We now live in a virtual world where men and women can flirt without having to shower, without having to groom themselves, and having the ability to lie about their past in a whole new medium.

Ahhhh... the Information Superhighway. Where would we be without Al Gore?

According to the U.S. Census, 100 million people are single. According to Match.com, 40 million Americans use online dating services, most of which are single as well.

However, there are some drawbacks with online dating, such as when you finally meet someone and they look nothing like their "recent" photo posted online, taken circa 1986 with a Polaroid.

These people should be sued for false advertising.

Further, people lie on their dating profile, just as people lie on their résumé:

"Sure, you were named most likely to become an Olympic gymnast before your untimely toe injury."

Since I'm such a logical and strategic guy, I even applied target marketing and utilized the Internet to help determine where I wanted to live the rest of my life. When deciding to relocate from St. Louis, Missouri, I asked myself *"If I could pick any city in the world to live, where would it be?"* I researched business factors, lifestyle factors, cost of living, and—of course—the singles scene.

While I zeroed-in on relocating to South Florida because of the climate and high propensity for thong bikinis, I didn't know anything about *exactly* where to live within the vast South Florida region. Just where do those attractive, young, single professionals reside? Of course, for something of this magnitude, I simply couldn't rely on the unscientific method of *"asking around."*

This was IMPORTANT. I needed FACTS. I needed MARKETING RESEARCH.

So, I undertook a 4-hour Internet research project using three separate online dating websites. I sorted my search by women ages 21-35, along with other ideal criteria, within 20 different South Florida zip codes. I tracked the findings, and identified a few zip codes which had several hundred matches, while

most other zip codes had less than 20. These findings were also consistent among the three websites.

I had my answers. Worked like a charm.

"Is it actually considered stalking if it's an entire GENDER that I'm hunting down??"

Legitimately, I really wanted to live in an area where I knew it would be easier to meet people my age and with whom I would have things in common. Let's face it, I didn't want to be stuck in a part of town where my Friday night entertainment consisted of *"Florida AARP Bingo Night & Charleston Contest."*

Chapter 14

CAPITALIZE ON SOCIAL MEDIA OPPORTUNITIES

It can definitely pay dividends to embrace our social media movement, whether it be with Facebook, LinkedIn, Google Wave, or Twitter (*the website formerly known as Stalker.com*). Sorry, just the thought of having strangers "follow me" 24 hours a day is a still a little weird.

Social media has indeed revolutionized communication. My Mom kept asking me what I was up to. I told her to follow me on Twitter.

However, in this constantly transforming virtual world, any of these social media sites might go the way of MySpace, if it's suddenly deemed "not cool" anymore by the powers who deem what's "not cool." For instance:

"If you're on Twitter, you're a loser." – Charles Barkley

So, we must stay in tune with the latest and greatest of interest to us, and always be ready to capitalize.

Marketing genius and social media stud Randy Gage, who has tens of thousands of followers on Facebook, Twitter, and a zillion other social media sites, offers a great example of providing a mix of value and fun to engage a captive audience. Randy also created *Tweet This: A Twitter Manifesto*, and subsequent sequel *The Twitter Manifesto Remix*, which outlines advice, rites of passage, and even comedic descriptions of not-so-beloved characters trying to spoil the fun of social media for everyone else.

Such spoilers include "The TMI Guy," who constantly keeps us posted on each trip to the bathroom (*and how it went*), and "The Food Dude," who constantly updates everyone on what type of sandwich he's eating (*and the factors behind choosing mayo over mustard on this particular day*).

My favorites are the Facebookers who ask me to become a "fan" of establishments such as "Al's Garage and Auto Repair," and those "too-much-time-on-their-hands" folks who find old classmates and excitedly quip *"Do you remember me? I sat behind you in 3rd grade!"*

Yeah, I remember you.

I didn't like you in 3rd grade either.

However, **continually building our database of contacts can bring endless benefits**, from getting a date, to getting a job, to landing a new account, to learning travel tips, or to get constantly spammed for the stuff everyone else is selling.

Don't try to compile a ton of "friends" and "followers" just to look good or boost your ego, like adding a school-full of 8-year olds from South Korea. Target relevant followers.

The real trick of capitalizing on social media is understanding how we can use such forums to provide value for relevant followers and engage potential customers with real problems.

So, how can you use your expertise or experience to help people, and draw people to you? How can you help people save money, improve their business, experience better health, or enjoy life more?

Engage people. Listen to them. Assist them. And more will come.

It is paramount to understand exactly where your potential clients are visible and interacting. Strategically, which social media sites, blogs, and listservs can you contribute to? Which sites will people want to hear what you have to say, will be taking notes, and will be passing your wisdom along to other friends and colleagues? Soon, you can gather a formidable following of those who respect what you have to say, and are interested in what you have to offer.

No matter your purpose, it's always important to make people smile. People interact on social media sites for a variety of reasons, but I believe one of the most popular reasons is to "escape" from the real world into the virtual world, if only for a few minutes on a mental break. Therefore, it's OK to share a funny thought in your head, such as when I tweet random wisdom such as:

"The most common first name in the world is Mohammed. The most common last name is Chang. However, the most common full name is not Mohammed Chang."

My colleagues and I enjoy contributing daily to our blogs and social media sites, which we like to think are a perfect mix of providing valuable content and comic relief to those stressed-out professionals (*and unprofessionals*) out there.

On a personal note, I've had the opportunity of reconnecting with countless old friends I would have otherwise needed a private investigator to locate (in fact, some of them *have* eluded private investigators). I've even been contacted by cool cats also named "Andy Masters" around the world who located me online and said "*Hi.*" Pretty neat.

In February 2009, Kelly Hildebrandt of Coral Gables, Florida, stumbled onto a namesake of hers on Facebook who lived in Lubbock, Texas. Except, this Kelly Hildebrandt was a guy. They chatted online for a few weeks, then decided to actually meet in Florida. Five months later, they were married. That's right. Kelly Hildebrandt married Kelly Hildebrandt.

I wonder what they're going to name their firstborn?

Kelly has a nice ring to it.

Chapter 15

Do Some RESEARCH ON YOUR PROSPECT FiRST

(WITHOUT BEING CONSIDERED A STALKER)

Indeed, in either business or dating, you should always do your homework first through a little surfing on your prospects before you meet them. In fact, an estimated 50% of singles have Googled their dating partner within the first 30 days of the relationship.

The other 50% wish they had.

Beyond just Google, you can often find incriminating photos of potential partners or prospects on Facebook, as well as the YouTube video clip of them hanging topless from a hotel balcony singing "Margaritaville." *(OK—I admit it. That was me. But those beads were worth it.)*

Of course, if a prospect is single, there is also a 40% chance you can find their profile posted with an online dating service—which can provide some real inside scoop for that next meeting.

"So, I hear you like romantic walks on the beach and snuggling on the couch listening to Barry Manilow. Me, too. Anyway, here is the contract for you to review and sign..."

You can also research online which associations they belong to, what college they attended, what previous companies they worked for, and all prior convictions. By the way, there are associations for absolutely *everything*, from the Greeting Card Association to the Cremation Association of America (*no word on whether those two collaborate on recycling efforts).* Check the *Encyclopedia of Associations* at your library for a listing of over 100,000 to dig into, and research those that fit your potential prospects.

Such research can also locate red flags about a person you are considering doing business with, as well. I once pondered an offer to work with a particular agent, until I Googled him and learned he had been expelled from the major professional association in my field for a "severe ethics violation." Along those lines, the Better Business Bureau website is always a nice reference to be sure your client will actually *pay you* for services rendered.

At this juncture, **it should be noted that others are consistently researching you**. So, beware… as turnabout is fair play.

In 2008, I presented a career development program for student-athletes at the NCAA Convention in Nashville, Tennessee. During the lunchtime panel Q&A session, I was alongside a Vice President for a coveted Fortune 500 Company. The executive was asked what the process was for checking references on candidates who applied to work for this company.

He stood up, grabbed the microphone, and stepped to the center of the stage to respond.

"Sure," he said. *"First we check your Facebook page, then we check your MySpace page, then we check your references."*

Faces of TERROR swept across the audience as if there was a wardrobe malfunction… suffered by Mick Jagger.

Beyond probing embarrassing photos or jovial curse words posted by friends and loved ones, let's not rule out a final step of due diligence on someone—with the authorities. A few of my police officer friends would occasionally run background checks on license plates as a favor for our single female friends. I suppose that can't hurt. If I were a woman, all of this research would be a prerequisite before any first date.

Then again, if I were a woman, I would look MUCH better in that red dress and heels in the back of my closet.

Further, you can go to: http://www.familywatchdog.us, and get a detailed map of where registered sex offenders reside within your zip code.

Try it. Who knows, you might even find one of your clients.

If so, you might want to schedule that next business meeting at a crowded, outdoor restaurant in the middle of the day.

You can never be too careful with so many dangers and pitfalls nowadays, even in the business world. In my first book for young professionals *Life After College: What to Expect and How to Succeed In Your Career*, I devoted an entire chapter to dating in the workplace, and sexual harassment (*that's avoiding it, not how-to*).

Of course, before we get too stereotypical, remember... sexual harassers can be female, as well. I know, because I worked with one of them. Angela... you GROPER! YOU KNOW WHO YOU ARE!!

NETWORKING:
IT'S ABOUT
RELATIONSHIP BUILDING,

NOT JUST CONTACT BUILDING

According to the book *Sex in America: A Definitive Survey,* 63% of married couples met through a network of friends—not as strangers in a bar or a grocery store. In fact, only 9 percent of women and 2 percent of men say they've found their relationship at a club.

Similarly, an estimated 65% of all jobs in this country are gained through networking and interpersonal contacts *(I suppose that leaves 35 % for nepotism)*. We must embrace the reality that networking is extremely important in all facets of business and life.

According to the prominent business and networking "Rule of 250," on average, every American knows about 250 people. This includes your extended family, friends, co-workers, previous co-workers, your neighbors, people on your softball team, college and high school classmates, and any undesired co-habitants.

Now, take just ONE of those people right now and picture them in your mind. Just ONE... such as that distant cousin in Georgia you don't even like that much. How many people, on average, does that one person know? **250 people.**

You might be thinking *"OK, I know 250 people, and they know 250 people—that's 500 people. That's a lot of people. I get it."* However, 250 people multiplied by 250 people equals 62,500 people in this world, just between who YOU know, and who THEY know. 62,500 PEOPLE!

Now, to illustrate one key principle of how we can expand the power of such networking, we turn to one of the single greatest movies ever made: *The 40-Year-Old Virgin*.

I must admit, I was SO excited and SO fired-up that Hollywood *finally* decided to make a movie on my life story. YES!!

Ok, Ok... while the lead character in the movie was also named Andy, I'm just kidding on that one. TRUST ME, folks... I'm kidding. I'll have you know, I am nowhere NEAR... 40 years old.

I actually did practice abstinence in high school, but it wasn't by choice.

Nevertheless, in one famous scene, the lead character Andy (*played by Steve Carrell*) was given advice on how to engage a single woman in a bookstore. His Cyrano de Bergerec friend, played by Seth Rogen, gave him one simple piece of advice: "Just keep asking her questions."

"Gold, Jerry... Gold!"

Applying that piece of advice to either a business or dating encounter could go something like this:

> "So, where are you from originally? Why did you decide to move here? That's great, what do you do for fun? Are you single? So, where exactly do you live around here? Do you live alone? What time to you get off work? What's your Social Security number?"

OK, I'm just kidding on those last few. But you get the point. Ask open-ended, conversation-starting questions about the other person... without looking like a convict.

Dale Carnegie provided us similar advice decades prior, as he said, **"You will gain more friends in two months from becoming interested in other people than you will in two years of trying to get people interested in you."**

This is especially profound for salespeople, as the biggest mistake salespeople make is BLABBING about the features, advantages, and benefits of their product, service, or company rather than LISTENING to the needs and wants of the consumer first.

People don't want to be sold to, they want to be listened to.

Beyond this lies the action step of "*What can I do for the other person first?*"

Don't bring a prospect, client, or colleague a brochure and squirt bottle with your company logo. Bring them a referral! Bring them something that's going to help their business. Bring them something that's going to make their life easier. Bring them something clever, useful, or personal.

Bring them promotional items with *their* company logo on it.

Let's say you opened up your contact database (*or prehistoric Rolodex*) and brainstormed how you could help just ONE contact per day for ten minutes. That's an honest, focused, and creative ten minutes where you stared at the screen and truly asked yourself:

"What could I possibly do within my power and imagination to help this person or their business?"

"Who within my 250 contacts could help this person, or would be in the market to buy their product?"

People need help with everything. Perhaps they need someone to volunteer for a committee, write an article for a newsletter, provide a discount on printing services, or give a babysitter recommendation. If you provided benefit to sixty people for sixty straight days, would you see a return on your (cost-free) time investment? Absolutely.

We must undergo a transformation from doing a job, to creating a bond.

Networking isn't about collecting business cards and asking for unearned referrals. Spend time truly helping others in business and in life, and it's amazing how much reciprocation will magically come your way. That's the true spirit of networking.

Chapter 17

CAPITALIZE ON THE **POWER** OF REFERRALS AND WORD OF MOUTH MARKETING

From that powerful network stems the MOST EFFECTIVE and LEAST EXPENSIVE form of advertising: **Referrals and word-of-mouth marketing.**

So, why do so many companies spend thousands, and even millions, in advertising and promotions without fully exhausting this avenue first?

Your best customers are also your best salespeople.

Every company and salesperson should build an army of people who are helping sell for them. Referrals can come not only from current and past customers, but also employees, friends, and colleagues in related fields. So, how can we maximize the potential of this sales army?

It's been said that everyone's favorite radio station is WIIFM – *"What's In It For Me."* Now, that isn't intended to be cynical. There are many who are willing to recommend without expecting anything in return—especially if they like you or your product/service. However, people are busy, and often have 900 billion things on their mind at any given time. We need to facilitate an encompassing program that asks for referrals, communicates incentives, makes it easy to refer, and offers periodic reminders.

So, what is your referral incentive system? What do you offer to the army of those who can truly help you?

☺ *Gift cards?*

☺ *Percentage of commission?*

☺ *Sending equal business back to them?*

☺ *Tickets to their favorite sporting event?*

☺ *"GREAT Job" smiley-face stickers used on 1st grade homework?*

Understandably, some industries do frown upon, if not ban, many referral "favors," "bird-dogs," and "kickbacks." But, fortunately for most salespeople, business owners, and elected government officials, these come in pretty handy.

So, what would they *really* want? What would really incentivize and reward someone?

We *think* everyone loves cash.

OK, just to clarify, everyone DOES love cash.

However, when I ran sales incentive programs for clients such as AT&T, Lexus, and Toyota with a major performance improvement company, we understood the magical value of *non-cash awards*. Different people are motivated by different things.

Don't just settle for that $100 check which will simply go towards someone's grocery bill. Make the other person treat themselves to one of life's pleasures that he or she wouldn't normally treat themselves to—which they will truly LOVE.

No matter the reward, I've always offered generous *"Thank Yous"* for people who refer my programs or help initiate a large volume book order. Why not? I appreciate every bit of help, and want to show my appreciation in return. I'm also eager to seek opportunities where I can send business back their way, as well. That's part of building those win-win relationships in business and in life.

Of course, the dating equivalent to this entire concept of referrals is having people "*set you up with*" someone. Such helpers in life could be friends, family members, co-workers, or mail order bride agents.

Married friends always seem to be great at this, because many are bored and miss the excitement of the "game." Therefore, the best they can do is to play matchmaker and live an exciting life vicariously through their single friends.

However, don't all these people need incentives and reminders as well?

Seriously, do you know how many times someone at a party, family function, or social event said *"Oh, I know someone who would be perfect for you!"* Or, *"We've got to find somebody for you. I have lots of single friends. Give me your card!"*

Then, what happens is: Hours turn into days. Days turn into weeks. Weeks turn into months. No calls. No e-mails. No anything. It's a whole new atmosphere of rejection.

Now, it's not because people are mean, or are just leading me on for fun. Again, people are busy, and have 900 billion things on their mind. But, most importantly, they lacked that incentive to actually follow-through. They lacked that same incentive we provide for our customers. So, then I thought to myself…

"Wouldn't it be great if…?"

Wouldn't it be great if I could utilize a referral system in the dating world? It would go something like this:

"Thanks, Aunt Pat… and I'd be more than happy to send you a $25 Gift Card to your favorite restaurant for any first date referrals you might send my way. No limit!"

Furthermore, since utilizing previous customers for referrals is so important in the business world, why couldn't we apply this concept in the dating world as well? That would go something like this:

"Julie, I'm really sorry it didn't work out between us. I wish you the best of luck. By the way, could you give me the names and contact information for 3 of your single friends that might be a good match for me? Thanks, I'd really appreciate it."

Chapter 18

BE WARY OF WHO PEOPLE SET YOU UP WITH

Unfortunately, counting on the world of referrals does have its drawbacks sometimes. What other people might believe is a good match for you might not fit *your* definition of a good match for you. Therefore, things could go South in a hurry.

My friend Mike once set me up with this person named Jennifer, whom he described as a *"Take home to Mom"* type of girl. Hmmm... if she was so promising, how come HE wasn't going out with her?

While I was very weary of blind dates to begin with, my leads were drying up at the time, and I had nothing else better to do that Thursday evening. So, I agreed to meet Jennifer after a brief conversation on the phone, which sounded normal. Further, I saw a photo of her, which also looked normal.

Then again, a photo of Jeffrey Dahmer looked normal, too.

Among the list of golden rules during an initial meeting is to avoid any conversation of politics, religion, and past bouts with HALLUCINATIONS and MULTIPLE PERSONALITY TRAITS.

Appropriately, it was the week of Halloween, and we met rather late at a neutral bar/restaurant for a drink and appetizer. After the first 10 minutes of typical chit-chat, I casually asked if she was into haunted houses, since there were a few nearby. Her disposition immediately turned to terror as she exclaimed:

Jennifer: *"Oh my Gosh—I HATE haunted houses. The last time I was in a haunted house, I was so tripping on acid, I totally thought the demons were jumping out to get me."*

Andy: *"Waiter... Check, please."*

Kiss Your Customer

Believe it or not, I actually reconsidered my idea to leave right then and there. My *"glass is half-full"* side convinced me to stay for some sick and twisted reason. Prophetically, I thought to myself this evening could be great material if I ever wound up writing a book on dating... or near-death experiences.

Indeed, my date with Jennifer (a.k.a. *"SHE-DEVIL"*), got much more creepy, but I'll just leave it at that.

I immediately called my friend Mike on the way home, highly unsympathetic about the possibility of waking him up late on a weeknight. I said *"Hey, Mike—I thought you told me this Jennifer person was a 'Take-home-to-Mom' type of girl? Whose Mom... Marilyn Manson's!?!?"*

Needless to say, I didn't take him up on any referrals for awhile. Or, until the next time I was desperate. Alright, IT WAS THE FOLLOWING WEEKEND, OK?

We've all had someone try to "hook-us-up" with great relationship leads that didn't pan out. We've all had someone try to "hook-us-up" with great business leads that didn't pan out, as well. You know, those anticipated meetings where you arrived thirty minutes early, only to ask yourself five minutes into the meeting *"What in the hell am I doing here?"*

Such dreaded encounters cause you to grasp your cell phone in a sweaty discomfort, while pleading: *"PLEASE someone call with an emergency. An important client. A telemarketer. A collection agency. ANYBODY!"*

Misguided referrals are also frequent when attempting to fill an open position. When I was a sales manager trying to expand our department, one of my top salespeople recommended a new hire to me, and *"vouched for his character."* His first day, we learned he had a warrant out for his arrest in another state. Thanks.

I didn't know my hiring of this fugitive now put ME in jeopardy for "aiding and abetting a criminal."

No hiring referral bonus for YOU this month, Brian.

Lastly, such fool's gold examples also include hook-ups with fantastic money-making opportunities.

Friend: *"Hey, I can set you-up with one of the TOP financial guys in the country, that even a bunch of celebrities use!"*

You *"Really?"*

Friend: *"Yeah. His name is Bernie Madoff."*

Do your best to pre-qualify such hook-ups in business and relationships, before just blindly trusting someone. Or, threaten to institute a penalty in exchange for a referral bonus, when the experience is so poor (or *life-threatening*), they should reimburse you for time and money wasted.

Chapter 19

CAVEAT EMPTOR
(LET THE BUYER BEWARE)

I've presented numerous programs for real estate professionals, who have always been dear to my heart since my mother was a real estate professional, as well. One powerful real estate doctrine which can be applied to many areas of business and life is *"caveat emptor"* (Latin for *"Let the buyer beware"*).

This shouldn't be confused with *"cave canem"* (Latin for *"Beware of dog"*), which is equally important in dating.

Ensuring the other party has full disclosure before any transaction is not only right, it saves both parties time and money. Some industries excel at such up-front communications with potential customers, while others require you to research the internet, call the Better Business Bureau, or resort to hiring a private detective to learn the real truth about a product or company.

Certainly, no other product or service provides a greater example of *"let the buyer beware"* than beloved pharmaceutical commercials. Of course, the lead-in includes brilliant qualifying questions such as:

"Are you between the ages of 18 and 90?"

"Do you find yourself getting tired every night?"

"Do you find yourself becoming hungry several times a day?"

"If so, then this product is for YOU."

No kidding. I can just envision the frenzy in every American household watching:

"Hey, honey... Get in here QUICK. This is just what we've been waiting for!"

This captivating audience-grabber is followed by 45 seconds of disturbing side effect warnings, described while showing a joyous couple flying a kite together over a beautiful beach:

"Contact your physician before the use of Traumatrol, as it may cause anxiety, depression, diarrhea, nausea, liver disease, enlarged glands, growth of a third eyeball, and in some rare cases your body exploding into a thousand pieces of burning flesh upon consumption."

Gee, thanks. Sounds like I'll need to contact my physician AFTER I take this stuff, not before.

If only every transaction in our lives gave us so much advance disclosure.

Wouldn't it be great if all companies would be required to provide full written disclosure of what might really happen after a purchase? I've survived customer experiences where the upfront disclosure from my salesperson should have read something like:

*"**Dear Valued Customer:** Thank you for your order. You will never see me again. Your product will arrive at double the time I just promised you. A part will break soon which is not covered by the extended warranty I also suckered you into purchasing. You will now begin your relationship with our Support/Service team. Our automated customer service menu (otherwise known as the Telemaze of Terror) is available 24 hours a day, unless you want to speak to a live agent, in which case you will hold for two hours before being connected with one of our foreign agents who won't be able to understand you anyway and have no empathy for your problem. If you decide you are dissatisfied and want to break this contract, HAHAHAHAHAHA! We have*

enough legal bindings in the fine print at the bottom of what you just signed, that you will be a lifelong customer unless you want to pay us the early release penalty, which is fine by us because we make more profit that way and don't even need to provide the service to you anymore. Have a nice day."

So, then I thought to myself…

"Wouldn't it be great if…?"

Wouldn't it be great if men and women had to give full written disclosure of all skeletons in their closet at the outset of a relationship? WOW, that would save people a lot of time, money, and misguided hope.

The standard disclosure questionnaire which both people should be required to bring on each first date would look something like this:

How many nervous breakdowns have you had in the last year?

Are you married already?

How many children do you have living in other states?

What medications do you currently take?

Over-the-counter: _____

Prescription: _____

Your brother's buddy "Dr. Feelgood": _____

Please list number of arrests here:

Misdemeanors _____ *Felonies* _____

What are you really like? Not just during the first three weeks of dating when everyone tries to be normal, but, for real?

Men:

Do you drink way too much on dates, becoming belligerent and hitting on other women?

Does your idea of a romantic Valentine's Day include ordering pizza and watching ultimate fighting on pay-per-view?

60

Women:

Will you take three hours to get ready while your date is waiting outside in the parking lot with the car running?

Will you become a possessive control freak who requires your man to wear an electric dog collar 24 hours per day?

Lastly, for the record, please state your real age. Really. Like, using an actual birth certificate. Not a copy, but an original signed by a licensed doctor at the time of birth.

If they did that back then.

If we aren't upfront with our propositions in life, we'll accumulate a long list of enemies who will hunt us down like a pack of wild dogs.

Chapter 20

SHARE TESTIMONIALS FROM PREVIOUSLY SATISFIED CUSTOMERS

The value of testimonials in business is vital, but most companies and salespeople either don't use them nearly enough, or don't use them effectively. Who better to say great things about you to future customers than your current and past customers?

People don't want to hear it from you. *That's selling.*

People want to hear it from someone else. *That's telling.*

The key to effective testimonials is that each is clearly from a person *just like your ideal customer*, who shares the same decision-making factors about your product or service. These are called "peer testimonials," such as:

"At first I was apprehensive about sending my kids to a new dentist, but after their first visit with Dr. Hart, they kept asking 'Mom—when can we go back again?'"

– Reba Williams, 37, Houston, TX

Testimonials also must be believable, and checkable using full names, titles, and cities. I immediately dismiss testimonials that end with *"From Joe S., Oregon."* Seriously, who signs their name that way, besides in *Penthouse* letters?

Another form of testimonials is *"expert testimonials,"* which are provided by a credible figure within the field. This could include an industry expert, company president, or even a celebrity who has used the product or service.

"I've been defended by many lawyers in my life, but none were more professional and diligent than Robert Shapiro. I wish I'd hired him for my last trial in Las Vegas!"
– O.J. Simpson, Inmate,
High Desert State Penitentiary, Indian Springs, NV

Testimonials are GREAT for the business world. But, of course, I've always wondered....

"Wouldn't it be great if... ?"

Wouldn't it be great if I could utilize testimonials in the dating world? You know, so prospects could obtain even more background information on me from women *just like them*—but who have already *"been there, done that."* This would be much better than saying good things about myself. That would be bragging.

Therefore, utilizing testimonials for dating would go something like this:

Andy to Prospective Date: *"I know you don't know me too well, and you might be apprehensive about dating me. So that's why I brought along a list of testimonials from previous relationships, written by women just like you."*

"Andy was the BEST boyfriend I've ever had. I highly recommend him to any girl looking for the man of her dreams!"
– Michelle Harvester, St. Louis, MO

"Andy is SO clever and funny. I'll never forget the purple plastic worm he gave me on our first date!"
– Dana Collins, St. Charles, MO

"After several therapy sessions, I've identified that Andy possesses many of the characteristics necessary for a successful relationship."

> – Dr. Jill Smith, Personality Disorder Therapist
> Plantation, FL

Believe it or not, I actually tried that once... ONCE.

Hopefully, your response will be more promising than mine, which was something along the lines of *"Get away from me, you FREAK."*

Ok, so maybe that's taking things a little too far. However, there is still a principle here. **Customers are much more comfortable buying from someone they've already heard something positive about. Women are much more comfortable meeting men whom they've already heard something positive about.**

There is definitely a concept called "testimonials-by-mouth," otherwise known as your *reputation*. Word gets around, for better or for worse... *especially* in business and relationships.

Chapter 21

DON'T SEEM TOO DESPERATE

So, let's say you meet this hot prospect at an event one evening, and get their phone number. They tell you they are interested, and want you to give them a call sometime. This person is JUST what you've been looking for! You are so excited, you want to call them at 7:00 am the next morning... you cannot WAIT! You can't even get to SLEEP that night!!

But then your logical side steps in. STOP. Calm down. Take a deep breath. Don't get carried away. The last thing you want to do is seem too desperate.

So, you calm yourself down, and start rationalizing why you should wait to call, and for how long.

But, what is the perfect amount of time to wait, where they don't think you are too desperate, but—where they also feel you are interested and value the opportunity with them?

Hmmm.....

This example could be **sales.**

This example could be *dating.*

According to a survey conducted by It's Just Lunch dating service, 97% of men will call within 72 hours to arrange a second date if they felt chemistry on the first date. This either means 72 hours is the "industry standard," or most men are too desperate to wait any longer. Ladies, if you are still waiting by the phone after that 72-hour window, you might want to pick up the phone to call the guy back—(despite the fear of looking desperate, of course).

According to *Merriam-Webster Dictionary*, "desperate" includes "*involving or employing extreme measures in an attempt to escape defeat or frustration.*"

Signs a person is too desperate for a sale include:

They purchase their own product out of pocket just to meet quota.

They enlist kids to hawk products door-to-door for sympathy sales.

They hold customers hostage with a semi-automatic pellet gun and exclaim "Buy this or I'll shoot."

Signs a person is too desperate for a date include:

They pass out business cards at divorce recovery workshops.

They wait outside the state penitentiary for female prisoners to be released.

They place an ad in the AARP personals asking "If still alive, please call."

Many are desperate for a date. Many are desperate for a sale. Yet, the important thing is to *not show it*. While this can be quite challenging, seeming desperate can be damaging, in either sales or dating. People are turned off by those who seem desperate. They start asking questions such as:

Why won't anyone else go out with you?

Why won't anyone else buy your product?

Why won't anyone else hire you?

What's wrong with you that everyone else knows about, but apparently I don't?

Acting desperate is the opposite of acting confident. Confidence is sexy, and good for business. Desperation is associated with low self-esteem. Low self-esteem is not sexy, and bad for business.

On the positive side, feeling desperate can create action resulting from a sense of urgency. Perhaps there is financial hardship during a tough sales month. Perhaps prom is only hours away.

Channel that sense of urgency through confidence, and never let 'em see you sweat.

Consumers want to buy from someone who is confident about them self, and confident about their product. Singles want to date someone who is confident about them self, and confident about what they have to offer.

However, there also needs to be balance, as there is a danger if confidence is too low, or too high. For instance, in the dating world, millions of women throughout history have expressed the feeling *"I like confident men, but not cocky."*

Low Self-esteem = Bad.
Confidence = Good.
Cockiness = Bad.

Self-esteem with men is a funny issue. Some men feel insecure and intimidated if a woman is more intelligent, more educated, or earns a higher salary. I feel insecure and intimidated if a woman is capable of beating the crap out of me.

This paranoia stems from an unfortunate misunderstanding between myself and my high school sweetheart which resulted in a brief trip to the emergency room—which will be discussed in greater detail in Chapter 69: *Create an Amicable Breakup.* This, along with several other traumatic experiences (such as earning a *1.66 GPA my junior year*) left me struggling with long bouts of wavering self-esteem in high school.

However, I underwent a major life and attitude transformation in college, which occasionally teetered on cockiness. I won several awards, made the Dean's List, served as Student Government President, and most importantly reigned as the 4-time defending foosball champion on campus.

Yeah...that's right. Foosball.

Trust me, nothing boosts your ego greater than slamming a little white ball past someone's unarmed goalie, and having everyone on campus call you "Wrists of Gold."

Life was good.

However, perhaps my most shining moment in college was posting two intramural soccer records that will never be broken: Goals per minutes played and shooting percentage.

While I played many sports as a youth, soccer wasn't one of them. It was always just a dream. So, I cheered on my intramural team from the sidelines all season long—until one day opportunity finally knocked at my door.

And, I was ready to answer.

After two critical injuries, and my team sporting an 8-0 lead with a minute left to play, I GOT MY CHANCE. This is when the greats rise to the occasion. This is when the stars seize their opportunity. Ringo Starr. Tom Brady. Gerald Ford.

And the rest was history.

Sporting a pair of jeans and black high-tops, I broke down the right sideline chasing a long clearing pass. I could run, so I tracked it down and saw an angle to launch a quick shot which snuck just inside the near post. BULLSEYE!

One minute. One shot. One goal.

There's no better feeling than putting the final nail in the coffin for your team in a big game. I still remember the screaming and delirious victory laps to this day. What a feeling. JUBILATION!

It was close though. The goalkeeper dove, but it just slipped past her extended left hand. Gotta love co-ed sports.

Needless to say, after my victory laps ended, I didn't get any phone numbers from the girls on the other team (sore losers).

And that was the end of my soccer career.

I was asked to play full-time the following year, but I declined. There's nothing like going out on top with a lasting legacy. It's someone else's record to break now.

In all seriousness, I realized something as I was running around the field screaming on that crisp Fall day. It was about confidence versus cockiness.

Nobody really likes cocky.

Confidence is an unwavering belief in yourself, and what you have to offer. As soon as your confidence spills over into cockiness, humility in life finds a way to knock it down.

Humility also has an impeccable sense of timing.

In business, it always seems I am humbled right after my peaks, and hit my peaks right after I am humbled. It's an amazing cycle that life brings us... in both our personal and business lives. I've been tremendously humbled, and now appreciate every ounce of good fortune that comes my way.

I believe people spend too much time worrying about the things they're not good at in life. *"I'm not good at sports. I'm not good with finances. I'm not good at this part of my job."* It brings us down.

Forget that.

I believe we should eliminate, delegate, lessen, or ignore the things which we aren't good at, and conversely channel our attention, energies, and emotions towards the things we are good at.

Find what you love and know what you do well. Then become happier, more confident, and achieve greater heights performing those things which bring the best out of you.

Chapter 23

JUST BE YOURSELF

It's easy to become consumed with constantly trying to be perfect. There is pressure to always be "on," always wanting to impress, and always trying to be everything to everyone.

So, perhaps the simplest and most effective piece of timeless advice in either business or relationships is to *"just be yourself."*

That is, unless you are schizophrenic. In that case, just be yourselves.

Being yourself is easy. It's natural, and you will put the other person at ease as well. Don't try to be someone you're not. That could be perceived as fake and artificial.

Are you being yourself, or are you being who someone else wants you to be?

I remember one night right after college, my desperate friends and I concocted this ridiculous theme for an evening out called *"Suit Night."* Twelve of us decided to scrape up money for a limousine, and we each dressed up in our best (or only) suit to hit the town for the most upscale restaurants and bars in the city. Our goal was to look as rich and as cool as possible, even though we were far from either.

Every time a group of attractive women walked by, one of us was responsible for holding our glass high in the air and loudly announcing *"Cheers everyone—Here's to our first million!"*

Dorks.

A few of us even printed up business cards for the night with fake titles such as "CEO," "Attorney-at-Law," and "Model Agency Director." A shameful and pathetic display that only rivaled the "Girls Gone Wild Video Crew" T-shirts that we—err—some friends I know wore one night.

Near the end of "Suit Night," however, one of our guys finally blew our cover when he "owned up" to one female about our charade. **Interestingly, he was the only one that garnered a lasting relationship from the evening.**

Hmmm…

I suppose we learned the moral that *"just be yourself"* wins.

Some people-pleasers in the dating world take trying to be a perfect match a bit too far. I mentioned to one date that I loved sports, especially football. She became excited and bragged about how she has been a HUGE life-long Green Bay Packers fan.

"Great," I thought. "Here's something easy to connect with during our conversation."

So, I told her how Green Bay Packers legend Vince Lombardi had been a great influence in my life.

She said "Who…?"

Then she tried recovering quickly by adding, "I'm sorry, I don't follow all the players' names and stuff." (For those non-football fans, Vince Lombardi was the Hall-of-Fame Coach of the Green Bay Packers for whom the Super Bowl trophy was named).

Don't try to be something you're not. It usually backfires.

I remember sales training at my very first full-time sales job. The company taught us the age-old technique in sales to mirror your prospect. If they speak slowly, then you should slow down, and vice-versa. This mirroring concept also includes mannerisms, and even body language.

Most of my potential clients in this job were small business owners in a very rural territory which I was assigned to. As an ambitious and creative young salesperson, I probably took mirroring JUST a bit overboard.

I pasted an NRA sticker in my car window and blasted Lynyrd Skynryd as I pulled into each appointment. The next thing I knew I was breaking out my Jeff Foxworthy imitation on them:

"Howdy, Partner... I'm fixin' to make you a deal today!"

Now, while I am from the Midwest, I'm also a lifelong city slicker who wouldn't know the difference between milking a cow from a bull.

Needless to say, they could see right through me.

"Son, you'd better high-tail it outta here before I tie your legs up like cattle and drag you up and down the road in my 4x4."

Ehhh... Thank you for your time, sir.

Much obliged.

Chapter 24

TIMING IS EVERYTHING

Even though we hate to admit it, deep within all of us there is a dark side. A dark side which possesses radar ready to take advantage of a given situation—prepared to jump on an opportunity when another is most vulnerable.

Perhaps a previous relationship just ended in disappointment, mistrust, or even outrage. A final straw has just been broken. But, in another person's moment of peril, there is a desperate hope. A desperate hope that someone out there could be their savior.

And that savior could be you.

So, you tell that person JUST what they want to hear, at JUST the right time.

That's right, you swoop in like a VULTURE to land that next two-year contract, OUSTING the incumbent who just blew their opportunity.

Truly, perhaps there is no better ally for a salesperson than perfect timing:

☺ *A car salesperson who witnesses a 10-car pileup right in front of the dealership.*

☺ *An insurance salesperson who walks in as the VP falls down the stairs at the company picnic.*

☺ *A roofing salesperson hired the day after a Category 5 hurricane hits.*

☺ *A syringe salesperson hired the day before a Grateful Dead reunion tour comes to town.*

Truly, perhaps there is no better ally for a single guy than perfect timing:

☺ *The moment after she watches Sleepless in Seattle for the 17th time.*

☺ *The moment after she finishes her 7th glass of wine and announces that her ride left without her.*

☺ *The moment after she learns her best friend is getting married and says: "Oh, I'm so happy for you." (No, you're not... you're more depressed than ever!)*

☺ *The moment after she catches the bouquet at her best friends' wedding. (For a full explanation of female vulnerability at wedding receptions, please refer to the movie Wedding Crashers)*

So, here's the question from a sales and marketing perspective:

How can we dictate, predict, or respond to periods where the potential for perfect timing is at its peak?

January 1st and July 1st are the two most common dates for companies and departments to receive new budgets. April 16th can be great if your target market is expecting tax refunds. If your target market just donated generously to Uncle Sam, run and hide.

Always consider the seasonality of companies you might be marketing to. Health and recreation products or services are great during the New Year, in conjunction with New Year's Resolutions. Holidays are great for many retail products, however, it's also peak season for suicide hotlines.

75

What about particular days and times of the week?

Contacting clients or prospects on Monday can be trouble because people are extremely busy, although it's also when people create their "To-Do" lists for the week. Fridays can be advantageous because there are fewer meetings scheduled, while people aren't as stressed about the week anymore and are generally in a better mood. However, it's also the most common vacation day, and people mentally check out after about 11:00 a.m., if they haven't left for the weekend yet.

Typically, people schedule meetings from 9:00–10:00, 10:00–11:00, 2:00–3:00, and 3:00–4:00. People are usually at lunch somewhere between the hours of 11:30–1:30. This means the best times to call clients or prospects are between 8:30–9:00, 11:00–11:30, 1:30–2:00, or 4:00–4:30.

Of course, the principle of "timing is everything" can go the other way, too.

Examples of really bad timing in the business world include:

- ☹ *Your boss walks in right as you are playing darts in your office... using his picture as the bulls eye.*
- ☹ *You get fired the day after you place a deposit on a new home. And a new car. And an engagement ring.*
- ☹ *Your prospect just learned their spouse had an affair with someone... who looks just like you.*

Examples of really bad timing for men in the dating world include:

- ☹ *Asking out a beautiful woman the day after she committed to a convent.*
- ☹ *Asking out a beautiful woman just before she announces "How coincidental... My Dad is your boss!"*
- ☹ *Asking out a beautiful woman just before she announces "Hi, my name is Kevin. My operation yesterday went GREAT."*

Chapter 25

LOCATION. LOCATION. LOCATION.

Indeed, the principle of *"timing is everything,"* does ring true. **However, so does the principle of *"being at the right place at the right time."***

Another classic real estate principle—*"location, location, location"*—is of utmost importance with many forms of sales and dating advice.

As a Marketing 101 refresher, the *"4 P's of Marketing"* include: 1. Product, 2. Price, 3. Promotion, and 4. PLACE.

There is a reason that commercials for Pampers don't air on ESPN, and commercials for Castrol Motor Oil don't air on Lifetime. Beyond common sense, it is based on legitimate marketing research. It is smart to strategically *"play the percentages,"* and play your game in the right ballpark.

- ☺ *If it's important to find a partner who is good with kids, volunteer with a youth organization or date a teacher.*

- ☺ *If it's important to find a partner who has strong religious beliefs of the same faith, go to singles events at your church.*

- ☹ *If it's important to find a partner who enjoys midget wrestling and quiche-eating contests, you're screwed.*

If an active lifestyle is your passion, ditch the smoky bars for singles activities such as rock climbing, horseback riding, and sailing with "Events and Adventures" dating service, found at www.lotsofevents.com.

Are millionaires your target market? Believe it or not, there's actually a dating website www.dateamillionaire.com (the website formerly known as www.Golddiggers.com).

Gentlemen, are "cougars" your target market? First, please keep in mind all cougars aren't as hot as Courtney Cox's character on ABC's *Cougar Town*. So, where do cougars in your area hang out *(besides the zoo)*?

Certainly, you can peruse websites such as www.dateacougar.com, or www.gocougar.com. But, did you know you can also attend none other than the National Cougar Convention? Why not aim for the top, and ask out Gloria Navarro, 42, who was named Miss Cougar America at the 2009 Convention.

Don't ask me why I have so much research on this.

Very early in my dating career, I had an ingenious philosophy to hit on girls while they were at work, because they couldn't run away from me. It worked GREAT!

If they worked in retail at the mall, for example, they were paid to be nice to people and talk to customers in the store. So, I knew my ego was a little safer there. They would at least have to smile and be polite before walking back to call security.

As I grew slightly more mature, I found attending young professional association events were great win-win situations, because I knew I had two chances with every woman in attendance. Either I could work on selling her my services, or selling her myself. Some environments can be great for meeting prospects of both sorts *(or can quickly double your rejection count)*.

One of my mentors once shared with me the three magic letters of successful salespeople and entrepreneurs: "*ABM—Always Be Marketing.*" Everywhere.

The airport. The grocery store. The street corner.

Just be careful on the street corner. People might misinterpret what services you're offering.

On that note, prostitution has been referred to as the "*world's oldest profession.*" However, if you consider ancient bartering as a sales job, then these would be the world's two oldest professions. Indeed, prostitutes and salespeople actually have a lot in common. I thought about writing the book *Why Salespeople Are Just Like Prostitutes*, but I didn't want flack from the prostitutes union about damaging their reputation.

Chapter 26

ALWAYS BE READY (YOU NEVER KNOW WHO, WHEN OR WHERE)

Since opportunities in either business or relationships may arise at any moment, we must always be ready. **We never know when we must make a great impression, and we never know when we must avoid making a very bad impression.**

So, how prepared are you when you step out to run those personal errands on the weekend?

Often in my programs, I display an article excerpt about convenient and casual dress which reads:

"Debra Jackson loves shopping at the Dollar Palace because it is convenient and casual. Debra explains: *'It's not like I have to get all dressed up like I'm going to Walmart or something.'"*

Wow.

I wonder what she gets dolled-up in for an extravagant trip to Macy's... a replica of Michelle Obama's inauguration gown?

By the way, have you ever noticed the Dollar Store is about the LAST place you want to run into someone you know? It pretty much ranks up there with the unemployment line and STD clinic. They should just hand out paper bags with eye-holes at the entrance so no one will recognize me—errrr, recognize you.

I was in the grocery store early one Saturday morning, and could have sworn I saw my financial advisor. During our meetings, she was always so perfect. Perfect hair. Perfect makeup. Perfect dress. I peeked again down the cereal aisle... and I just *knew* that was her.

Except... WOW did she look bad!

You know how some women don't need makeup in the morning to look beautiful?

Well, she wasn't one of them.

My interest rate in her sure went on a sharp decline. She looked as if she had just crawled out of bed either sick or hungover, and left her house with no makeup saying "*Gosh, I hope I don't run into anybody I know.*"

Sound familiar?

She had to have seen me—I know she did. But she avoided any eye-contact, and was determined to do whatever it took to escape any confrontation. She desperately dove from the end of the cereal aisle to behind the produce stand, taking cover between the cantaloupe and grapes. Scoping me out. Peering through the vines.

Waiting.

Waiting.

Waiting.

I thought it was pretty funny, but I also felt sorry for her. I felt kind of sorry for the grapes, too. So, rather than listening to my sadistic side by fondling through the cantaloupes just to torment her, I left her alone, and acted like nothing had happened the next time I saw her.

Many people are able to "turn off the switch" once they leave work. They live by the concept: "*This is an 8-hour job, not a 24-hour job.*" That is actually a healthy outlook to a certain extent, helping leave stress and work problems locked behind those office doors. That's great.

However, *you never know*. **You never know when you will run into a current client, past client, or future client. Or, perhaps even the next love of your life. Your image is always on the line as soon as you step out of your house. 24x7.**

Chapter 27

SOMETIMES THE BEST OPPORTUNITIES COME WHEN WE LEAST EXPECT

Becoming obsessed about achieving our goals can place an unhealthy amount of stress on ourselves, and everyone else we come in contact with. **Such stress can become a barrier to realizing the exact prizes we covet.**

There have been countless success stories about consumed businesspeople who were forced to put life into perspective first.

There have been countless love stories about obsessed singles who decided to just stop and enjoy their lives first.

And, that's when it happened.

A good friend of mine, Christopher, had suffered through many disappointing relationships, and sensed his window for finding Mrs. Right was closing. He was finally convinced by friends that he was placing too much pressure on himself, and to focus on work and having fun first.

So, he did.

One morning, Christopher was running late for work. It was raining, traffic was horrendous, and all the decent parking spots were already taken. He finally parked his car and ran across the street, zig-zagging downtown traffic to reach his office building.

He didn't make it.

A Chevrolet SUV struck Christopher just before he reached the sidewalk in front of his tower. His right leg was broken, as was his collarbone, and his shoulder was dislocated. An ambulance soon arrived with help.

Along with a beautiful young paramedic named Kylie.

Christopher couldn't believe he had met someone so kind, caring, and unselfish—as she continued to check up on him days after the accident. Kylie couldn't believe she had met someone so strong, kind, and sincere.

The couple were married less than 18 months after that painful day.

I remember Christopher joking afterwards *"My other relationships all ended in pain. This one began with it!"*

Fate and serendipity often have impeccable timing.

A good friend of mine, Jason, works in an unforgiving pressure-cooker sales job with a mid-size cleaning supplies company. In the midst of the recession, the sales staff in his region dwindled from five to two, with the other remaining rep being the son of the President. Jason was understandably worried he could be next to go, which would be crushing as he was struggling to support his wife and two young girls as it was.

Salary had been dismal for months with Jason's predominantly commission sales job, and the financial walls were closing in. In addition to an impending layoff, their mortgage was in danger of not being paid again, and a potential bank foreclosure loomed.

However, Jason had a long-standing vacation scheduled for a family trip to Disneyland, and the time for this promised trip had finally arrived. You simply can't break promises to 5-year old and 3-year old daughters. The show must go on.

Jason, his wife Jessica, and his daughters Cassidy and Amber, got settled in for their flight, which he upgraded to first class using airline points.

Jason leaned to Jessica and shared:

"I feel like I shouldn't even be here. I should be back home calling every broker and purchasing agent in the Midwest from dawn to dusk. I feel guilty even being on vacation. I don't even deserve a vacation. It's not like I'll be able to enjoy it, anyway.

You really should have just taken the girls on your own, so you three could enjoy the trip."

His supportive wife leaned over and replied:

"Jason, everything will be alright. Somehow. Okay? But, please Honey—whatever you do, please try to relax and enjoy this week's vacation. It's so important to the girls. They feel like they never see their Daddy anymore because he's always working. Okay?"

Indeed, Jason undertook the most therapeutic exercise he knew of to get his mind off work and financial pressures. He sat his 3-year old daughter in his lap and read her Disney stories one after the other, making her laugh with his funny cartoon voices along the way.

Amber looked up and said "You're so silly, Daddy! I love you."

"I love you, too... Sweetheart. I love you, too," Jason replied with a tear in his eye.

A man seated behind Jason and his family overheard the entire story during the flight. When they landed, he handed Jason a business card and said:

"Don't worry about this now. Just call me when you get back to the office next week. Enjoy Disney with your family first," he said with a smile.

The title on his Fortune 500 business card read:

"Vice President – Purchasing, North American Division"

Upon return from Disneyland, Jason landed the largest account of his career. It saved his job, saved their mortgage, and even helped save his company. Jason was a hero to his co-workers, but most importantly to his family.

"A man should never neglect his family for business." – *Walt Disney*

Sometimes when life priorities are jarred into place by the unexpected, *life rewards us* with the unexpected.

FAILING TO RISK IS RISKING TO FAIL
(DON'T JUST STAND THERE WITH YOUR HANDS IN YOUR POCKETS)

Indeed, principles such as being in the right place at the right time and the power of serendipity, can offer magical opportunities. However, we also can't fall into a trap of simply trusting fate in our lives.

Sometimes fate needs a good kick in the butt.

The day after I wrote the previous chapters on fate and serendipity, I was presenting a program which required me to drive through rural northeastern Texas. As I drove east on I-30 outside Dallas, I approached a sign which read "CITY LIMIT: FATE, TEXAS."

I started to smile.

Then, to my amazement, less than 100 yards later I approached another sign which read: "CITY LIMIT: ROYCE CITY, TEXAS."

What? Fate, Texas had the shortest city limits of any city I had ever seen!

Then I smiled again as I had one of those "Aha!" moments in life:

Fate has a very small window.

While fate is a friend, fate only *presents* us with brief moments of opportunity in life. Often, opportunities are also disguised as risk.

So, what can we learn about both business and relationships... from turtles? No, not to take things slowly. A turtle is the only species that doesn't get anywhere in life without sticking its neck out.

One day I was walking into a Subway shop at almost the exact same moment as a very attractive female. I, of course, opened the door for her, and followed her inside to the "Order Here" counter. The employee looked up at us both and said, "*Are you two together?*"

I quipped back "*I wish!*" with a smile.

That quip definitely caught her off guard, as she looked at me like I had a piece of molded salami hanging from my forehead.

Not exactly the response I was looking for.

I would have preferred something along the lines of... "*Your first wish has been granted, Mr. Masters. How would you like to utilize your final two wishes?*"

Hello!

Back to reality, I never saw that woman ever again. I shot, and I missed.

So what?

"*There was never any fear for me, no fear of failure. If I miss a shot, so what?*" – Michael Jordan

In my younger days, I became so angry with myself when an opportunity came and vanished, while I just stood there with my hands in my pockets. I finally had a revelation that I would rather deal with fear of failure, than live a life overwhelmed with missed opportunities. In fact, that's not living a life at all.

I never regret taking risks anymore. With anything.

I believe most people are afraid to take risks in life. People are too often victims of *"What If? Syndrome":*

- ☹ "What if they say no?"
- ☹ "What if nobody buys it?"
- ☹ "What if it doesn't work?"
- ☹ "What if they don't like me?"
- ☹ "What if her Dad finds out?"

Action is taken when the desire of the outcome becomes greater than the fear of failure. The happiest and most successful people are motivated by their desire, not squelched by their fear of failure.

Wayne Gretzky once said: *"I missed 100% of the shots I didn't take."*

Babe Ruth once said: *"I never let the fear of striking out get in my way."*

Britney Spears once said: *"With love, you should go ahead and take the risk of getting hurt… because love is an amazing feeling."*

Ahhhh, the romantic visions of Britney and Kevin Federline sharing their fairytale bliss just brings a tear to my eye.

I believe life itself is a high-risk, high-reward proposition. Too often we accept the safe and standard route, rather than challenging ourselves beyond our comfort zone to pursue a different and perhaps risky route. I believe *"Safe = Sorry,"* rather than *"Better to be safe than sorry."*

Magical opportunities come our way throughout our lives. When one does, we have two choices: We can grab that opportunity and run with it, or we can keep watching it go by.

Sadly, too many *"err on the side of caution"* with such opportunities in life.

Key word: err.

YOU'VE GOT TO LOVE THE THRILL OF THE HUNT

Whether in sales or dating, our goal is to get the other person to say "*Yes.*"

That is, unless the question you are asking is: "*Would you like me to go away?*"

So, do you love the "*game*"? Do you love the challenge? Do you love bringing out your best to impress the other person? Do you love the thrill of the hunt?

In a roomful of "*hot prospects,*" do you break into a salivating frenzy like a lion stalking their prey?

Do you love getting the sale, not just for the money, and not just for the sales numbers, but just to get the sale? Just to get the other person to say "*Yes!*"

There is an adrenaline rush like no other when we get a "Yes" in life. I've always likened the thrill of the sale to scoring a touch-down, hitting a home run, or accomplishing any other feat on your favorite sports video game. Each "Yes" help us love life, and love our job.

My favorite Chinese philosopher Confucius once said:

**"If you find a job you love,
you will never work a day in your life."**

Of course, that was easy for him to say, since his job was to sit under a tree all day and think up clever proverbs.

Nevertheless, are you currently working at your absolute dream job? Do you work for the perfect company, in the perfect city, in the perfect industry which makes you happy? Do you love what you do?

We must enjoy the thrill of the hunt in our lives, no matter what that hunt is.

Sadly, there are too many examples of "accidental salespeople," and all other "accidental occupations" in this world, where the job chose the person, the person didn't choose the job.

"How did I even end up in this industry, anyway?"

I truly believe the happiest and most successful salespeople in the world were born to be in sales. For everyone else in sales, it's just a job.

Is this what you were born for?

"The two greatest moments of any person's life are the day one was born, and the day one realizes why one was born."
– Mark Sanborn, Author/Speaker

Often, it's just as important to identify what definitely does not make us happy, and what we are definitely not good at. This enables us to ultimately zero-in on our ideal life and career through process of elimination. Blindly continuing to labor 365 days per year attempting to push a square peg into a round hole isn't a career, it's unfortunate.

Fortunately, we have the power of choice in our lives. If you could pick any dream job, what would it be? What's your passion? Where would you work if you could work anywhere in the world, making a GREAT living doing something you LOVE?

- ☺ Working as a motivational speaker for underprivileged youth?
- ☺ Working as your own boss by starting that company you've always talked about starting, but never have?
- ☺ Working as the SCUBA diving instructor at the Atlantis Resort and Casino in the Bahamas?

☺ Working as an "Ice Cream Taster" for Ben & Jerry's, which was featured in a *Men's Journal* article: The 50 Greatest Dream Jobs (And Here's How You Can Get One)?

☺ Working as the personal massage therapist for Beyoncé? *(By the way, someone right now IS Beyoncé's personal massage therapist. Impossible is nothing.)*

If your answer is "NO" to each of the above, and "YES" to the exact position you hold now... AWESOME.

If not, for every career, there is a career path. Learn what individuals currently possess your dream job. Where do they work, and how exactly did they get there? Research it, target it, and join them. Do you need to earn a certification? Do you need two years of experience within a certain industry? Do you need to network your way into one of the Top 10 companies in the industry? So be it.

You get what you ask for in business and in life, and you can ask for anything you want.

What are you asking for?

Chapter 30

BE ASSERTIVE, NOT AGGRESSIVE

Surveys repeatedly confirm that women are turned off by aggressive men.

Surveys repeatedly confirm that customers are turned-off by aggressive salespeople.

Men are repeatedly advised by friends to "*Get out there and be aggressive!*"

Salespeople are repeatedly advised by managers to "*Get out there and be aggressive!*"

Sounds like a bit of a quandary to me.

Levels of sales aggression certainly vary by industry. Time-share folks, door-to-door salespeople, and Kiosk pushers at the mall are known to be more aggressive. That's because, for the most part, each have "one-time" sales opportunities, as opposed to long-term relationship building opportunities. They have one shot, and that's it... whether it's a good fit or not.

Could you envision, say, a pharmaceutical rep with the same aggressiveness as one of those warriors?

Rep: "*Look, Doc... I don't care, I don't care. Just listen. This is the GREATEST product ever. No matter what, you MUST start having every patient try our Viagra TODAY!*"

Doctor: "*But, I'm a pediatrician.*"

That would make some parents HIGHLY upset.

You know, *"Hey, how come WE didn't get any?"*

Have you ever noticed when you are shopping and don't want to be bothered, salespeople are all over you? But, when you have a question or want to have someone check in back for something, you can't find anyone?

Sometimes I feel I need a bullhorn to announce *"HELLO, I need an aggressive salesperson out here, please. I have wads of money falling out of my wallet and need some assistance!"*

Nevertheless, there is a difference between assertive and aggressive (*though both are better than AWOL*). One definition of assertive, according to Dictionary.com, is *"having a distinctive or pronounced taste or aroma."*

Gee, thanks. That helps.

OK, below are some signs I feel are more helpful to determine whether aggressiveness goes overboard in either business or dating.

Signs a salesperson might be too aggressive in the business world:

You "help out" by reaching into the customer's purse to grab her credit card for her.

You crack your knuckles and say "It sure would be a shame if something bad happened around here."

Your customer returns 20 minutes later with a police officer carrying a Taser. And a cavity search kit. *"Don't taze me, bro!"*

Signs a guy might be too aggressive in the dating world:

She arrives for a 2nd date accompanied with a bodyguard named Butch.

You steal her keys so she can't leave and are arrested for false imprisonment.

You slam an axe into her front door and announce *"Here's JOHNNY"* à la Jack Nicholson in *The Shining*.

Chapter 31

METICULOUS PERSONAL HYGIENE— IMPORTANT!

Admittedly, I am somewhat obsessed when it comes to germs and personal hygiene. I had no less than a dozen friends who urged me to see the film *As Good As It Gets*, because I am supposedly exactly like Jack Nicholson's OCD character in the movie.

Whatever. At least he got Helen Hunt in the end.

To illustrate the point, I have never even drunk out of the same glass or eaten off the same plate as any girlfriend in my life. GROSS!

They all thought that was weird, especially since I had no problem kissing them, among other things. However, they shouldn't have taken it personally. I don't even eat after myself. I know where my hands have been.

Further, some people are offended with my now famous *"sanitizer squirt"* right after an initial handshake.

Clients. You can never be too safe.

By the way, an automatic hand-blow dryer for public restrooms has to be the worst invention ever. I think every patron in the history of modern bathrooms has turned it on for about 10 seconds, said *"to hell with it,"* and wiped their hands on their pants as they left. Just for fun, check underneath these disgusting "bacteria blowers" after your next tinkle.

I'll just stick with my pant leg, thank you.

Nevertheless, when it comes to business or relationships, everyone should be aware of the unwritten rules of personal hygiene. Wash those hands. Brush those teeth. Trim those nose hairs (*otherwise known as nasal shrubbery for some, who should just hire a lawn service*).

Of course, one of the other unwritten rules of dating is if you are scheduled to meet the same person on two consecutive nights, a minimum requirement is to at least SHOWER and CHANGE CLOTHES between dates. My friend Chris must not have read that unwritten rule.

In his defense, there is no book on the unwritten rules of dating. Our educational system doesn't teach us this kind of insightful wisdom, either. **It's not easy for guys to be clean on consecutive days without proper training.**

After a marathon weeknight date into the wee hours, Chris crashed in his car, only to be awakened a few hours later by the sunlight, and an officer tapping on his windshield. It was 6:45 a.m., and his shift at the bank started at 7:00 a.m. With no hope of driving home and back to work in morning traffic, he spruced up with his emergency stash of deodorant and hair gel from his glove box. He somehow survived the day without notice or incident from bosses, clients, or co-workers (*fortunately for him, he doesn't look that good on a normal day, anyway*). Right after work that night, he met me for our scheduled happy hour at a nearby Macaroni Grill.

Chris was giving me the play-by-play on his previous evening's date, when suddenly his cell phone rang. It was her. After a quick conversation, he hung up and said, *"Guess what— that was Jill. She's stopping by here in 10 minutes. You get to meet her!"*

I said *"Dude, you haven't even been home to shower yet... SICKO. Tell me you at least changed your shirt in the car."*

That's when the look of terror struck his face. *"Oh, crap! Ohmygosh... What the hell am I going to do now?"*

Being the quick thinker and life-saver friend that I am, I told him to hurry-up and follow me into the men's bathroom. I had an idea.

Thank God the bathroom was empty, so we hurriedly began switching our shirts in front of the sink counter.

Right at the moment we both unzipped our pants to tuck in our shirts, the restaurant manager walked in. We looked up at him and froze.

Bewildered, he said *"Gentlemen, please leave the facility."*

I've never questioned my orientation more than at that moment.

Needless to say, the cat didn't stay in the bag too long when Jill arrived. Chris was wearing my oversized shirt that didn't match, complete with my company logo. Furthermore, since I'm 3-4 inches taller than Chris, with a wingspan of 7-8 inches longer, I looked like a total GOOFBALL in his shirt. Not to mention, it smelled like cheap cologne and had a snot stain on one of the sleeves.

But, HEY—what are friends for? It's happened to all of us.

Lessons learned: Whether in business or relationships, ALWAYS keep a spare shirt in your car for emergencies, NEVER schedule impromptu meetings if you are still wearing the same shirt as the night before, and be careful what public places you get caught with your pants down. By the way, Chris is now a Vice President at that same financial institution. God Bless America.

Chapter 32

FOLLOW UP.
FOLLOW UP.
FOLLOW UP.

In either business or dating, having the ability to follow up is first predicated on getting an actual phone number (the RIGHT one). Sometimes, that can be a challenge:

Man: *"I'd love to call you sometime. What's your number?"*

Woman: *"It's in the phone book."*

Man: *"But I don't know your name."*

Woman: *"That's in the phone book, too."*

Many optimists believe that if we give someone a card, everything should be OK. The other person now has your contact information and they told you they will call you back soon.

SUUUURRRREEEE they will.

NEVER trust anyone who takes your card and says they will call you. That's for SUCKERS! Always capture the other person's contact information, enabling you to control the communication exchange—forever.

So, what if the other person avoids your follow-up calls?

Don't worry, I've been there. Especially with dating, the three most common recordings I would hear included:

"Sorry, I can't get to the phone right now."

"Sorry, I'm either on the phone or away from my desk."

"Sorry, you've either reached a number that has been discon-nected or is no longer in service."

In either business or dating, leaving voice mail sucks. If the other person actually does call you back, it interrupts you when you're not ready. Just keep trying to catch the other person, and try calling from different phone lines so it doesn't seem harassing when your number keeps popping-up on caller ID. I've called from phones with separate area codes to really throw them off.

If the person you are trying to reach still won't answer your calls, request through your phone provider that the caller ID registers as "MOM" on all of your outgoing calls. That will catch them off guard at least once.

In sales, we often have the challenge of *"getting past the gatekeeper."* The gatekeeper, of course, is most often a secretary or some relatively unimportant person who screens calls and visits for the important person you really want to talk to. Always be nice to the gatekeeper, which may include thoughtful chit-chat on the phone, or donut deliveries for the staff during an office visit.

The best times to catch a decision-maker are before office hours open, at lunch, or after office hours have closed. That's when the gatekeeper is not around, so the phone might be picked up by the important person directly, or a substitute who isn't properly versed on how to screen calls for the important person. It's also highly advantageous to locate the direct extension of your targeted contact using the after-hours phone directory, company website, or my favorite free information assistance operator called Google.

With relationships, depending on the age of the person you are dating, the gatekeeper might very well be her DAD. This is bad, because Dads have a much better chance of possess-ing FIREARMS than most secretaries. Fortunately, single guys today have a great advantage over single guys 20+ years ago. Females now have personal cell phones. That's right, no more uncomfortable calls to the home phone and asking *"Hi, Mr. Jackyl—Can I talk to Meghan again, please?"*

Always have a reason to call someone—not to just bug them on if they've made a decision yet. Perhaps something new has just arrived, something has just been announced, or you've just received a great review from a client *just like them.*

There are a lot of advantages to email. People can respond at their own convenience throughout the day, rather than being interrupted by a phone call. Time and space aren't limited, so you can include helpful links, detailed information, and attachments into an email. I probably support direct email (*not SPAM*) more than others in the industry, but it depends on your style, what you are selling, and ultimately what has proven to be the most effective with your prospects and clients (*through tracking and research*). I'd take email over voice mail any day, though, that's for sure. Voicemail is for suckers!

Preference of method aside, what's paramount is that you actually follow up.

If you don't follow up, it creates the impression you're either disorganized, you don't care, or you're insulting the importance of the other person.

Following up in a *timely manner* is equally paramount. This is especially important in dating. Gentlemen, just give up on desperately calling a number back after you discover it cleaning out your nightstand drawer a year-and-a-half later.

"Hey, Nicole, remember me? I got your number last year at the Suds Shack. Sorry I haven't called you back yet, but I've had a few relationships since then. By the way, what do you look like again? I have a THREE written on the back of your card, but I don't remember why."

CLICK.

Chapter 33

DON'T BECOME TOO NERVOUS OR STRESSED OUT

The most profound quote artist in history, the ancient Greek philosopher Anonymous, once said:

> *"Stress is when you wake up screaming and you realize you haven't fallen asleep yet."*

Indeed, stress and anxiety can cause a multitude of negative side effects. Twitching. Shaking. Nail biting. Cursing. Random acts of violence.

However, everyone is required to perform some job in a certain amount of time, with a certain amount of quality. There's no such thing as a stress-free job (*except for a security guard at a nursing home, perhaps*).

So, what keeps you awake at night?
What are you stressed about?

- ☹ What about my sales numbers?
- ☹ What about my competition?
- ☹ What about the economy?
- ☹ What about world peace?
- ☹ What about those photos of me on Facebook?

I believe there are two types of stresses in life: Those we can control, and those we cannot control. If we are stressed about something we can control, we must identify all alternative courses of action, choose the best action, and take action. We must "zero-in" and focus. For items which we cannot control, we must "zero-out," as these worries serve no purpose—while stealing time, focus, and positive energies from other items which we do have control.

If there are many items in life which cause us stress at once, we must isolate our stress. We can't address everything at once.

The second-most profound quote artist in history, the ancient Chinese philosopher Proverb, once said:

"He who chases two rabbits for dinner will go hungry."

Pretty wise.

Although, I'd probably go hungry anyway, as I'm not a big rabbit eater, myself.

Beyond that, there are daily therapeutic exercises which can help relieve stress. Take deep breaths. Take five minute breaks. Go for a run. Have a stiff drink. Take narcotics.

And remember, stressed spelled backwards is *desserts*.

Nervousness is a related cousin of stress, but usually comes just before important short-lived moments or events in our lives. People become nervous before first dates. People become nervous before presentations. People become nervous before tests *(especially urine tests and pregnancy tests)*.

I had a friend in college who stayed up all night trying to study for his urine test, and still failed.

If we continually face our fears in life, we will slowly become desensitized to that which makes us nervous. Join Toastmasters. Try out jokes during open-mic night at a comedy club. Ask someone out just for practice, even if you don't like them. Walk down the hallway all alone in the DARK.

I've always been asked if I become nervous before programs, and if I have any tips for people on speaking in public. I had always heard *"picture your audience naked,"* but that just got me too excited.

Know your audience, establish rapport with your audience, and break the ice by making people laugh. It loosens the audience up, as well as yourself.

I often try to learn plenty about my audience at the outset by asking for a show of hands on a few basic questions, such as:

"How many people in the audience are in sales?"

"How many people in the audience are in management?"

"How many people in the audience are married?"

I would then follow with *"I don't have a point with that last question, I just wanted to identify who the SINGLE WOMEN are in the audience."*

Dating is another story. I could be speaking in front of 2,000 people on one evening, but would be 10 times more nervous before a first date the following evening.

THAT IS CRAZY!!

It's not that I'm not confident, or don't know what to say *(fortunately my dating cheat sheet helps me out with that)*. But we are judged on entirely different criteria. For instance, I have confidence in my words. I don't have confidence in my hair.

I possess one of those mops which decides what it wants to look like each day, with little input from me.

I remember during a TV interview for the NBC affiliate in West Palm Beach, I was more worried about my hair because I knew the camera was on my bad side. COME ON. Couldn't that cameraman see I had an Alfalfa-sized cowlick over there?

Another occasion, I was the 30-minute guest on an early morning business program, and the TV producer approached me and said:

"One minute until airtime. How are you doing? Are you nervous?"

I replied *"Yeah, I've got a hot date tonight. Do you think this makeup will last me until 7:00?"*

Thank God for Revlon.

If we keep laughter in our life, isolate our stress, and address only which we can control, we'll increase our chances for success and decrease our chances for a strait jacket.

Chapter 34

DON'T EMBARRASS YOURSELF

*"Samson killed a thousand men with the jawbone of an ass.
That many sales are killed every day with the same weapon."*
– Greek Philosopher Anonymous
(I told you that guy was good!)

In Dan Seidman's terrific book and newsletter *Sales Autopsy*, a must-read in the world of sales humor, Dan documented this embarrassing exchange of flattery gone wrong:

Salesperson: *"How did you get a picture of yourself with your arm around John Madden?"*

Company President: *"That's not John Madden. That's my wife."*

Yikes.

Better tiptoe right on down to the next prospect on your list.

One evening during a monster college party, I was shooting hoops in the back driveway and attempting to conquer my dream of dunking. With music playing, adrenaline flowing, and my Reebok Pumps pumping, I had never been higher-jumping. So, my good friend Charlie threw me one perfect alley-oop pass allowing me to jump—and for the first time in my life—SLAM IT HOME, BABY!!

I was EUPHORIC!!!

Except... nobody saw it.

So, I yelled inside to get everyone into the backyard to watch me do it again, including this cute girl named Jen I had the hots for. The music stopped and an announcement came over the loudspeaker:

"Everyone off the dance floor and proceed to the backyard. Andy Masters will be attempting to dunk in exactly 5 minutes."

With the crowd chanting and cameras clicking, my 15 seconds of fame had arrived. A star was born.

Well...

Unfortunately, let's just say my second attempt wasn't quite as graceful as my first. The alley-oop pass from Charlie was WAY off target *(THANKS A LOT)*, so I tried to look cool by grabbing onto the rim, slinging my legs high into the air, and letting go... which began a free-fall splatter to the concrete.

Witnesses claimed they heard my bones break from 100 yards away. I broke my wrist in 5 places. I broke my elbow. I broke my pelvic bone. I hyper extended my big toe. I suffered a grapefruit size hematoma on my hip. I passed out.

That moment reminded me of those Southwest Airlines commercials *"Wanna get away?"*

"Yes... FOREVER!!!"

Since Jen was one of the closest to me during my Evel Knievel plunge, she rushed to my aid and accompanied me to the emergency room.

I was still in agony at the hospital, especially after the doctor gave me a shot of some unknown medication. I just remember yelling *"What did you give me, Doc—PAIN ACCELERATOR?!?!"*

Needless to say, I was miserable and embarrassed.

The silver lining, however, is that I indeed got the last laugh. I dated Jen for the next year-and-a-half.

Ahhh, the Florence Nightingale effect. Works every time.

However, my goal in life from that point forward was to try to impress women WITHOUT having to break every bone in my body to do it.

I wonder if this Florence Nightengale effect works with potential clients, too? That'd be a tough way to make a sale, I suppose. No word on if ending up in a body cast increases your closing percentage.

I don't plan on researching that firsthand anytime soon.

Chapter 35

IDENTIFY THOSE RED FLAGS EARLY

When a female begins her conversation with *"You're cute. You remind me of my 3rd husband,"* it might be time to scoot on down the bar to your next suspecting victim.

Sometimes in life, a red flag isn't quite so obvious, and may not rear its ugly head for weeks. One afternoon, I walked into my condo building to stop by the front desk, and there was an unexpected guest. It was the woman I had begun dating just two weeks prior. She didn't stop by to surprise me, nor to bring me flowers or candy, which would have been nice. She was with her real estate agent, and said she was *"just in the neighborhood to check out the vacant East unit on the 15th Floor."*

"Oh, really?" I thought. *"That's pretty interesting since I live in the EAST UNIT ON THE 16TH FLOOR."*

Ok, that was a bit beyond coincidental.

Can you say *FATAL ATTRACTION*? Can you say *BASIC INSTINCT*? Can you say *ANY OTHER SPOOKY MICHAEL DOUGLAS FILM THAT FITS*?

I was so spooked, I only dated her for another three weeks.

But, that was it.

In the sales world, most salespeople try to identify red flags with a customer as early as possible so they can act accordingly, such as pawning them off to the rookie salesperson.

Customer: *"Yeah, right… that's in my price range… as soon as we win the LOTTERY!"*

Salesperson: *"Let me see if Joey is available to help you out."*

Having the ability to identify red flags can come in handy in many areas of business. Most hiring managers are adept at identifying such red flags within the first five minutes of any interview. I remember arranging an interview with someone whose résumé boasted *"love working with people," "great team player,"* and *"terrific interpersonal communicator."*

He possessed the social skills of Borat.

It's always a red flag if the greatest qualities a candidate can highlight at the top of a résumé consist of unquantifiable gibberish *(otherwise known as soft skills)*.

I always think to myself *"Great, you possess soft skills. Maybe we can do happy hour sometime. This is a business. What have your wonderful soft skills PRODUCED?!?!"*

Monster.com highlighted a list of actual interview answers which created red flags the size of Texas, such as:

☺ One applicant for an office position was asked how he would cut and paste in MS Word. He responded *"with scissors and glue."*

☺ One applicant was asked what brought him to this company, and he responded *"Oh, I drove here."*

☺ One applicant for a computer technician job was asked if there was anything he didn't like to do. He responded *"I don't like to clean my bathtub."*

☺ One applicant was asked on the application if he had been convicted of any crimes. He responded *"Yes, a Mr. Meanor."*

☺ One applicant was asked on the application of his race. He wrote *"Human."*

Lastly, take 3rd party opinions from people you respect to heart. Often, others can see red flags in situations where we are blinded. For instance, my college sweetheart wasn't the most

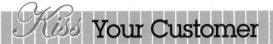

popular person with my friends. Proof? My nickname for her was *"Hon,"* short for *"Honey."* Within two weeks, my friends' nickname for her was *"Atilla the Hon."*

They were right, and I took it to heart. Eventually.

We broke up a year-and-a-half later.

I should have acted on those red flags earlier.

Chapter 36

TAKE THEM
SOMEWHERE
UNIQUE
and FUN

Over the last several decades, there has been a trend in sales events, corporate meetings, and employee trainings. People want to go somewhere fun, do something different, and experience a unique environment *(transvestite clubs NOT included)*. **People want to get excited about attending an event, as opposed to dreading it so much they create excuses to skip it.**

While bad PR from the recession put a damper on those extravagant Caribbean junkets, some basic principles learned about effective events will live on.

Unique and fun environments get people out of their routines, and open up people's minds. The same old lunch meetings are so uncreative, as are the same *"dinner and a movie"* dates. So passé.

So, what can you do on that next date or business meeting that your competition isn't doing? Where can you take your important person that is unique and fun?

In one episode of the hit TV series *The Office*, the office was persuaded to go ice-skating to celebrate the birthday of Michael Scott *(played by Steve Carell)*. Nice idea. The only problem is, Michael was the only one in the office who knew how to ice-skate. Not fun, and not necessarily safe for everyone else, either. In another classic episode, the team went to a campfire and walked on hot coals as part of a team-building exercise. Sounds great. A corporate liability lawyer's dream!

In the real world, avoid taking your top prospects anywhere too dangerous, such as swimming with the sharks or skydiving. It's pretty tough to complete a sale if they are DEAD.

Perhaps much safer than swimming with the sharks and walking on coals is golf and miniature golf. While "real" golf is better for the business world because there is plenty of time to make deals in between holes, miniature golf is better for dating. It's more entertaining, and much less of a chance it will ignite any rage *(except for the time I slammed my putter right into that clown's teeth).*

I would also give the obvious piece of advice to let the other person win, but I'm just a tad too competitive for that. Besides, if I lose—I'm in a REALLY bad mood the rest of the night, and that's not fun for either party. Therefore, it's win at all costs.

Hey, in the words of legendary race-car driver Ricky Bobby, *"If you ain't first, you're last!"*

I must admit, women look at me a bit strangely during my pre-game stretch and practice routine using different colored putters, but it's worth it.

I have a list I keep with me at all times called *"The South Florida Top 37 Fun List."* It provides 37 great ideas for my days off, for out-of-town visitors, and of course for sales and dating ideas. Included on the list are the most fun activities, clever hotspots, and scenic restaurants in South Florida. You should be an expert on all such places in your area, too.

There are always fun places such as Dave & Buster's, theme clubs, or any restaurant with live music, ambience, and environment. **Anything with atmosphere is a must.** Whether it's in sales or dating, go somewhere with energy and a crowd, but not somewhere too crowded. Just as in my favorite Yogi Berra line:

"That place is so crowded, nobody goes there anymore."

Check out the community calendar online, or in your local paper. There are always outdoor events, concerts, art exhibits, or some new establishment which has just opened up. Of course, one nice benefit of making this part of your business schedule is you can enjoy all of these attractions on the company's dime. Just make sure that unique and fun is also coupled with safe and appropriate, and aligns with their interests—not just yours.

Chapter 37

ELIMINATE YOUR COMPETITION (BY HAVING NO COMPETITION)

I've always hated walking into a place with plenty of good-looking women, only to look around and see even more good-looking MEN. I hate competition.

Go Away! Go Away! Go Away!... DIE! DIE! DIE!

Yeah, I know this country was founded on our great free-market system. Competition is good. Competition is healthy. Competition brings out the best in us. Blah-blah-blah.

However, when it comes to the mate-race, I'd sure like my chances if our planet suffered a peculiar gender-specific epidemic which left 4 billion women on the planet, with only ME to choose from.

I'd attempt to repopulate the human race as best I could. :)

Unfortunately in both business and personal relationships, we also compete with all previous experiences and relationships an individual has ever had. Such previous experiences mold an expectation of what future experiences should be. Often, those predetermined standards can be tough to live up to.

I dated one female who continually referenced her previous boyfriend throughout our dates and conversations. Her previous boyfriend also happened to be a bodybuilder and model, who even served as the stand-in for Hollywood hunk Dolph Lundgren in some movie.

Gee. Thanks.

Off to the gym I go!

Shortcomings aside, we must possess confidence that what we have to offer is better than what the competition has to offer. We all have gaps. But, so does the competition.

This reminds me of the profound wisdom Sylvester Stallone shared with us in the movie *Rocky*. When asked why he and Adrian were a such a good match, he explained in his slow, grumbling Rocky voice:

"I don't know. She's got gaps, I got gaps. Together we fill gaps, I don't know."

So romantic. I love chick flicks.

Perhaps we aren't good cooks, or we could be more patient, or we need to shower more often, etc. The list is endless—there are no perfectly chiseled human beings. Everyone has their strengths, and everyone has their faults.

Confidence comes when your strengths lift you higher than your faults bring you down.

For two consecutive summers, I taught an M.B.A. level Marketing Strategies course at Lindenwood University in Missouri. The first day of class, we would discuss that one of the most important roles of any marketer is to identify the strengths, or *"differentiated value,"* of a product or company vs. the competition. The job of a marketer is to SCREAM to its target market what that *"differentiated value"* is.

Right now, there are those within your target market clamoring for the strengths you possess.

Of course, the best way to beat the competition is to have no competition. So, other than employing a mafia-style strategy for eliminating your competition, what can you do to separate yourself from *"they all look alike"* syndrome?

Ideally, you want to separate yourself so greatly from the competition, that you have *no competition*. Each day should be a full-throttle mission to run as fast and as far away as possible from the word commodity. The ultimate goal is that no one can offer the exact same product, service, or experience as you or your company. Not even close.

What you offer is completely unique.

I was presenting this exact concept during my program *"Why Client Service Is Just Like Dating & Relationships"* in Riverside, California. The event was hosted at the historic and unique Mission Inn in Riverside. Why is the Mission Inn historic and unique? Among other things, it boasts exclusive artwork, internationally-inspired architecture, and daily tours. Richard and Pat Nixon were married there. Ronald and Nancy Reagan spent their honeymoon there. Bill Clinton enjoyed a scintillating rendezvous there (*OK—just kidding on that one... as far as I know*). Amelia Earhart, Charles Lindbergh, and John Glenn each have inscribed copper wings at the hotel's *"International Shrine of the Aviator."*

And, that's just for starters.

The point is, historic and unique doesn't just happen. A local hotel visionary named Frank Miller undertook a mission to create an experience so different, it would have no competition.

He was successful.

The Mission Inn has no competition. If you stay in Riverside, you either stay at the Mission Inn, or you don't.

So, how can you create a product, company, or experience so unique, *you* have no competition?

Chapter 38

I once read this wise saying on a bathroom wall:

Love like you've never been hurt.
Dance like no one is watching.
Sing like no one is listening.

Of course, this wisdom was trumped by a sign inside the stall which read "*Patrons Are Asked To Remain Seated Throughout The Entire Performance.*"

I know. Bathroom humor.

Nevertheless, don't be normal. Normal is boring. Be original and memorable. If you want to be like everybody else, do what everybody else does. However, last I checked, striving to be like everyone else doesn't seem all that aspiring.

Most Americans can't name either of their Senators.

Most Americans can't locate the state of New York on a map.

Most Americans don't read a book after completing their education.

So, as individuals, how can we stand out from a crowd with *anything* in life—and have FUN doing it?

When attending St. Louis Cardinals games at Busch Stadium, I always wear a blue shirt, even though our team color is red *(unless we're playing the rival Chicago Cubs)*. Why?

Two reasons: First, the color blue brings out my eyes. Second, my blue shirt helps me stand out in the crowd amongst the sea of red, making it easier to be seen on TV.

Cheesy? Probably.

However, friends seated across the stadium can easily spot me, I consistently see myself on evening highlights, and I was featured in a front page photo on *ESPN.com*. Further, I can also be seen if you freeze frame the final scene of the movie *Fever Pitch* with Jimmy Fallon and Drew Barrymore, which was filmed at Busch Stadium during Game 4 of the 2004 World Series *(I'm still upset about not being listed in the credits)*.

So, there.

Standing out in the crowd can also mean standing out in the crowd... on a busy dance floor. I'd be remiss if I didn't mention my now famous Michael Jackson impersonations in this chapter. That's right, all I need are some mirrored 80's sunglasses, a white left-hand glove, a red sequin jacket, and it's like I'm being possessed by the late, great King of Pop himself. The injury-risking transformation is complete with breakdancing, moonwalking—and of course—the obligatory crotch-grab.

Viewer discretion is advised.

Now understand, I don't break that out just anywhere—only on special occasions. Special occasions which include wedding receptions filled with hopeful single women.

Yep, works like a charm.

That is, if you consider being escorted off the dance floor by the bride's father a charm.

"Not at my daughter's wedding, Jacko—Back to Neverland Ranch you go!!"

That's OK. I saw the looks on those bridesmaids' faces. Oh, yeah. They wanted me.

Especially the one who said: *"Who's gonna 'Beat It' now, DORK?"*

I know that's just code for *"I hope you're the one who catches the garter, and I'm the one that catches the bouquet."*

The eternal optimist.

I once sailed on a Caribbean cruise with three friends circa 1992, and two of us decided to perform in the big talent contest by creating a skit impersonating Ross Perot and George Bush *(the first one)*. My friend nailed famous Bush lines such as *"read my lips"* and *"it wouldn't be prudent,"* while I wore HUGE plastic ears and kept barking in a high-pitched Perot accent *"What in the Sam Hill is that?"*

It was so much fun, and the crowd LOVED us!

But, somehow, we only took 2nd place. We couldn't believe it. The girl who went after us won. Geez... people acted like they've never seen an opera singing 5-year old juggle bowling pins while tap-dancing before.

Judges.

HIGHWAY ROBBERY!!

After we inexplicably lost our protest on the grounds that she CLEARLY went six seconds over her allotted time, we reluctantly accepted our 2nd place trophies and enjoyed the rest of our seven days of fame as *"George"* and *"Ross."*

So, what celebrity can you impersonate? What color can you wear to your next sporting event? What Wet T-Shirt Contest can you enter? *(I've STILL yet to win one of those).*

Have FUN in life! It will facilitate a mindset that you are truly an original and completely unique from everyone else.

Such experiences can also create a mindset which allows you to think differently in business, and create solutions in an entirely fresh and new way. People gravitate to those who enjoy life, and who stand out in a crowd. Significant others, friends, co-workers, and customers.

GET THEM TO COME TO YOU

My good friend Scott Ginsberg, author of several books including *The Power of Approachability* and *Get Them to Come to You*, has become a beacon of light for those wanting to stand out in a crowd in business and life.

Scott has also gained plenty of international notoriety for wearing a nametag 24 hours a day... for over 3,500 consecutive days... and counting. And, to ensure he also has showers and trips to the beach covered, I accompanied Scott while he gripped my hand in pain receiving a permanent "Scott" nametag tattoo on his not-so-sexy hairy chest.

Yep. It's true. Look him up.

However, over the last several years, Scott has acquired incredible marketing and interpersonal wisdom from his experiences, which he has shared with *CNN, 20/20, The Wall Street Journal, USA Today,* and even *The Today Show...* in Australia. *(Don't they think we're weird enough already?)*

I recall one of the first evenings Scott and I went out together. It was GREAT. Women were so intrigued that he was standing there wearing a nametag in a bar, that one after the other were continually coming up to us *(well, OK... coming up to HIM)*.

It was pretty funny to watch. Some women were nice and struck up a conversation with him. Some women made fun of him. One woman was belligerent enough to walk straight up and pull the nametag right off his shirt, saying *"What are you going to do now, Mr. Nametag guy?"*

He responded by calmly reaching into his wallet, pulling out one of his many emergency spare nametags, and slapping it right back onto the same place—with a smile.

However, the point isn't what women were coming up to him to do. **The point is that women were coming up to him.**

So, then I started thinking: *"What could I do to get women to come up to me?"*

I could wear a nametag also, but that would be unoriginal. I could wear a sign which reads *"WILL PAY CASH FOR DATES,"* but I tried that in high school already.

Ultimately, I learned it isn't so much about what signs we wear physically, but rather what signs we give off figuratively.

How does the opposite sex perceive the signs we give off?

How do potential customers perceive the signs we give off?

How do co-workers perceive the signs we give off?

How do family members perceive the signs we give off?

How do strangers perceive the signs we give off?

Do strangers feel enticed to greet you with friendly conversation, or do they clutch their purse with two hands and move swiftly away in panic?

What does your aura scream?

Are you approachable?

On a larger scale, how can we attract volumes of customers to come to us, rather than having to hunt them down through direct marketing and other stalker-like tactics?

When people search for the product or service which you provide, customers should find YOU. Immediately, and consistently.

So, what would your customer Google? What book would your customer buy? What article would your customer read? What blog would your customer contribute to? What seminar would your customer attend? Who would a friend refer your customer to?

What if it was your website they found through Google?

What if it was your book they found on Amazon?

What if it was your article they read in their trade magazine?

What if it was your blog they contributed to?

What if it was your seminar they attended?

What if it was your name that was referred to them by a friend?

It's called transforming yourself from a salesperson to an expert through personal branding. So, what is your niche? What knowledge can you package and share with others? How can you become "*the one to go to*" for your area of expertise?

How can you get them to come to you?

Chapter 40

BE A GREAT LISTENER

According to a survey conducted by It's Just Lunch dating service, 47% of U.S. women are turned off by men talking about themselves and not paying attention to their dates.

So, I suppose the other 53% don't mind?

Nevertheless, you get the point. People want you to listen. People want you to relate. People want you to understand. People want to tell you a problem, and hope you have the answer.

And, often, it's not even required that you have an answer. You just have to let the other person vent.

The first key to being a great listener is having the ability to ask questions—and not while you are also watching television, which you have strategically placed over the other person's right shoulder. The act of simply asking questions shows that you care about the other person's feelings, and are interested in the other person's life.

However, it's not just about asking questions. It's about asking the right questions. As with flattery, the quality of the question is a reflection of the person asking the question.

Begin with excellent conversation starters, which are original, not boring. Avoid closed-ended questions, or a question they could answer with *"Fine," "I dunno,"* or even worse, *"No."*

We want to ask questions which place us in position to be a great listener.

"What's the best vacation you've ever had?

"What's the best Halloween costume you've ever worn?"

"What's the worst thing an ex-boyfriend ever did to you?"

Perhaps even more important than asking good questions is to avoid asking dumb questions.

Dumb questions in dating include:

"How about this weather?"

"How much money do you make?"

"If I told you that you had a hot body, would you hold it against me?"

Come to think of it, those questions don't work real well in business, either.

Dumb questions are asked in business every day. I travel quite often, and must admit I'm tired of the same boring and predictable question whenever I arrive, "So, how was your flight?"

I always think to myself: "I'm not DEAD am I?"

I know, I know... that's a bit harsh. They could be wondering whether the flight was rough or if I was squished between a sweaty fat guy and a screaming two-year old.

I do appreciate the concern, but as we all know, I have a much greater chance of death being trampled in the mall the day after Thanksgiving.

Certainly, some questions are OK to ask in the business world, but not necessarily appropriate to ask in the dating world, and vice-versa:

Questions OK to ask in the business world, but not the dating world:

"Do you take credit cards?"

"I'm in a hurry. Can we speed this up?"

"Will your wife be waiting for you at home?"

**Questions OK to ask in the dating world,
but not the business world:**

"Do you consider yourself high-maintenance?"

"So, what are you wearing underneath that dress?"

"Chocolate really turns me on. What about you?"

Chapter 41

KNOW HOW TO INTERPRET NONVERBAL COMMUNICATION

It's been estimated that 80% of interpersonal communication is nonverbal communication, which can include body language, facial expressions, hand gestures, or violent physical attacks. The ability to interpret such nonverbal communications can help alter your game plan to best suit the thoughts and feelings of others. In the business world, this is also an example of possessing *"emotional intelligence,"* or EQ.

Examples of nonverbal communication in business include:

- ☹ If a customer places your number on their call-blocker, they probably don't appreciate your telephone persistence.
- ☹ If a customer marches away towards your manager, they probably didn't appreciate your ice-breaker joke.
- ☹ If a customer bursts into tears and runs towards the exit, they probably didn't appreciate your honesty in answering *"Does this look good on me?"*

Examples of nonverbal communication in dating include:

- ☹ If a single woman holds up three fingers and says *"read between the lines,"* that's probably not a good buying signal.
- ☹ If a single woman pulls out her can of pepper spray, you might have taken that grinding dance move during *"Funky Cold Medina"* a little too far.
- ☹ If a single woman takes off her shoe and throws it at your head, that probably means she didn't appreciate you invading her territory *(I believe G.W. Bush can confirm that interpretation for us, as well).*

Men frequently utilize codes and nonverbal signals within loud and crowded singles environments. Such signals have encoded instructions such as *"Go away, I'm working it,"* or *"Help get me out of this conversation!"* The most popular example of speaking in code is the always effective *"Hottie at six o'clock."* This instructs the other person to inconspicuously rubberneck around 180-degrees, before turning back to concur *"Yeah, she's hot...",* and resuming the conversation.

Attempts at such nonverbal signals can be confusing between men and women, especially when women don't utilize the same signs. One evening I brought a date to the loudest and biggest club I had ever seen. This place was the size of Vermont. She was trying to tell me something while waiting in line for the bathroom across the dance floor, but I couldn't hear her. I kept yelling *"What... WHAT?!?"*

Finally, she patted her mouth three times and pointed to the right.

I couldn't tell if she wanted me to get her a drink or steal third.

So frustrating.

Life would be so much easier for everyone if women would just tell us what they want in writing. Thank God for text messaging.

In sales, we must be able to determine right away if a customer is getting antsy, if a product is out of their budget, or if deep down they actually want to buy—but just haven't been asked yet.

Retail statistics show the most common response when approached by a salesperson in the mall is *"just looking."* (By the way gentlemen, this is probably NOT an ideal response when approached by an attractive female in the mall.)

So, what does "just looking" actually mean? It varies from customer to customer, often defined by nonverbal signals. In such situations, we need to read those nonverbal signals and make adjustments accordingly. We should be masters of this, and be constantly striving to improve our *"EQ."*

Unfortunately, we can't get through life only processing written statements, and we can't take verbal communication at face value. The *"people"* side of business and life are what separates the successful from the not-so-successful.

Chapter 42

DEAL WiTH THE FRUSTRATION OF GETTING MiXED SiGNALS

(IF WE COULD ONLY READ THEiR MiNDS)

One of the most frustrating challenges with reading people in either business or relationships is trying to process mixed signals.

Some people just can't make up their minds. Some people have their minds made up, but enjoy playing games. Some people sincerely dislike shooting someone down or telling someone the truth, so they lie, stall, or drag it out. All of these lead us on and give us false hope.

So, we simply lie awake every night wondering:

"She loves me. She loves me not."

"He's buying from me. He's buying from me not."

Some people enjoy playing games intentionally. Call it trying to get the upper hand, playing cat and mouse, or playing hard-to-get. I think most women preferred playing hard-to-get with me. Really hard. I met one girl who played so hard-to-get, I think she enrolled in the Witness Protection Program.

But, I hunted her down.

"You can run, but you can't hide, baby!"

Kiss Your Customer

Playing games is not only unfair, but such a complete waste of time, for both sides.

That reminds me of one of my favorite hit songs from the late 1980's, *"Straight Up"* by former Laker Girl, Paula Abdul. Yep, a true American idol. You remember that chorus line: *"Straight up now tell me do you really want to love me forever, or are you just having fun?"*

Now that I have your feet a tappin'...

> *"You are so hard to read,*
> *You play hide and seek*
> *With your true intentions*
> *If you're only playing games*
> *I'll just have to say*
> *Bye, bye, bye, bye, bye, bye, bye, bye..."*

I remember when I grew out of playing games. It was when I turned 30. From that point on, I simply said *"Hey, we either like each other or we don't."*

This straightforward method sure made life a lot simpler.

Since then, I've just put people on the money, not only in life, but in business. In sales, this saves time from having to bug the other person, and saves the other person time from getting bugged.

There are plenty of other fish in the sea to bug.

Too often, salespeople are afraid to ask for a definite answer. This stems from fear the answer might be *"No."* Therefore, inaction lingers. Such inaction with so many prospects eventually mushrooms into an unmanageable pile of *"maybe someday's."*

Perhaps some people sleep better at night with a huge list of *"maybe someday's."* Hope of 1,000 sounds better than hope of 200, I suppose. But, if each *"maybe"* of the remaining 800 is really a *"No"* in hiding, false hope is wasting valuable time.

Each salesperson should attack their *"maybe"* database, and achieve either a YES or a NO.

Both accomplish something: A *"maybe"* which turns into a *"Yes"* makes money. A *"maybe"* which turns into a "No" doesn't waste your time anymore.

In business, the more you put people on the money, the more money you make from people. Games don't pay the bills.

Chapter 43

MASTER PERSUASIVE COMMUNICATION, THE ART OF NEGOTIATION, AND THE ABILITY TO COMPROMISE

Have you ever been to a third world country and been approached by locals trying to sell you products or services on the street? Wow...they are good! With no formal sales training, either. They are assertive risk-takers who have confidence in their product, are persuasive, and have the keen ability to negotiate on the spot.

And, that's just the prostitutes and drug dealers.

One afternoon, I had just completed my program at the American Leadership Academy which was hosted in Cabo, Mexico (*I still haven't figured that out—must have been a NAFTA thing*). I decided to share lunch with a few colleagues at a nearby outdoor patio. We were approached by this child selling bracelets, who couldn't have been more than 5 years old. He was so darn cute. I was just compelled to engage him in a lighthearted exchange. Fortunately for me, he spoke good English, since the only Spanish I remember from college was "*Yo quiero Taco Bell.*"

I said: "*How much for the bracelet?*"
The kid said: "*Ten dollars.*"
I said: "*Ten dollars? Hmmm.....*"
He said: "*2 for 10.*"

I said: *"2 for 10? Hmmm....."*

He said: *"3 for $10 or 4 for $15."*

I repeated back to him: *"3 for $10 or 4 for $15—Wait a second, wait a second."*

Then I slowly repeated to myself: *"3 for $10...OR...4 for $15...?"*

I've got two frickin' Masters degrees, and now needed a calculator to keep up with this kid. I looked around the table for some quick mathematical help, and all I received were blank stares and shoulder shrugs in return. Thank God we were at least dealing with dollars instead of pesos.

William Shatner, the *"Priceline Negotiator"* himself, would have been proud of this South-of-the-Border Eddie Munster.

Finally, I turned back to him and said:

"OK—Give me 4 bracelets."

So, I just gave him $20 and added:

"If these break, you'll be hearing from my lawyer."

He smiled, and said: *"Muchas gracias, Señor!"*

"Muchas gracias," **I replied as I smiled back.**

Sometimes likeability can go a lot further in negotiation than slick sales lines.

The most profound statement I've ever heard about negotiation is this: **The side with the power in any negotiation is the side that has the ability to say "No" and walk away.** Very true, and very powerful.

I know from dating experience.

In business and in relationships, we must keep our competitiveness in check. Is the goal *"Win"*? Or, is the goal *"Win-Win"*? It's healthy to employ a mindset that the other person isn't the opponent, but rather represents part of a larger team who is striving for a common goal along with us.

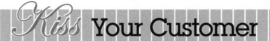
I've always searched for any conceivable win-win propositions in business. What is the true motivation of the other person? Money? Time? Quality? To look good for their boss? To make their life easier?

**Understand the true wants and needs
of the other side, negotiate accordingly,
and help them win, too.**

Chapter 44

DEAL WiTH FEAR OF COMMITMENT

As a man who has grasped on to single-hood for 38 years, I feel qualified to speak on fear of commitment.

The only time I felt comfortable uttering the "L" word was in a sentence describing admiration for my favorite sports teams.

"I LOVE the Cardinals!"

The only time I felt comfortable uttering the "M" word was in a sentence describing my favorite sitcom reruns.

"The show *Married With Children* is hilarious!"

I remember the first time I went shopping for an engagement ring back in my early 20s. Panic attack... BRING ON THE OXYGEN TANKS!!

I just kept hyperventilating while gasping at the sky pleading: *"Elizabeth, I'm coming to join you... this is the BIG ONE!"* (That's a *Sanford & Son* reference for you young whippersnappers out there).

Are you familiar with the *"scared straight"* effect? Well, this was the *"scared single"* effect. Indeed, it wasn't a good sign when my first question to each jeweler was *"What's your return policy?"*

One salesperson asked me if I was familiar with the "4 C's" of a diamond. I replied *"Absolutely. Commitment – Commitment – Commitment – and Cost!"*

I know, I know. I should have looked forward to a wedding day. After all, it's a special day most people only get to experience a couple times in their lives.

Ha.

Believe it or not, as a best man, I actually recited that sarcastic line to the stressed-out bride on the eve of her wedding to loosen her up.

It didn't work.

Sorry, Renee!

Finally, I can't even commit to the responsibility of owning a pet. I had a pet fish once, but my Dad killed it. "Wags" was a victim of an unfortunate ammonia cleaning accident. I was so scarred, I haven't been able to own a pet—or touch cleaning supplies—ever since. At least that's my story, and I'm sticking to it.

Of course, I'm not alone when it comes to such fear and paranoia about commitment. **People in relationships, as well as consumers, often struggle with the ability to finally say "Yes."**

So, why is that? At the heart of commitment issues, people are afraid of feeling *"locked in."* They feel the pressure of the old cliché *"there's no turning back."*

Questions which constantly harass someone right before committing to a major decision include:

"Am I making the right choice?"

"What if I change my mind?"

"What will other people think?"

"What if a better opportunity comes along?"

"What if 5 or 10 years from now, things don't look the same as they do now?"

Despite many of these paranoid concerns, most bachelors decide to take the plunge, anyway.

Most paranoia is based on F-E-A-R, which stands for *"False Evidence Appearing Real."* To put someone at ease before a major commitment, remind them of another time they made a major commitment and it worked out well for them. Help the other person understand that taking no action can often be worse than taking any action.

Pose the question: *"What's the worst thing that can happen?"* (Unless their answer could be *"We could go bankrupt and land in jail."*)

Change, risk, and commitment are an ally to happiness. People must take action today to be happier tomorrow.

Whether that's committing to buying a new car, signing up for guitar lessons, or finally approaching the person they've had the hots for.

IDENTIFY THE OBJECTIONS AND OVERCOME THE OBJECTIONS

One of the most important skills in sales is having the ability to identify customer objections and overcome those objections. **The first step is to simply identify the true objection, which can easily be half the battle.**

This is similar to a relationship when someone asks the frustrating question to a pouting partner *"What's wrong?"* The partner might stubbornly mumble a response such as *"Nothing"* or *"I'm fine."* Which, as a wise friend once told me, F-I-N-E stands for *"Feelings – I'm – Not – Expressing."*

These responses usually accompany a crossing of the arms, a turning of the head, or even a pushing-away of a full dinner plate. It's like dealing with a two-year old. A two-year old can be crying and pouting—and you want to help them—but you just have to get out of them WHAT IN THE HECK IS WRONG. You can't help them if you don't know what's wrong.

The worst response to overcome in either business or relationships is *"I dunno."* If you have an *"I dunno,"* you have nothing. You have no chance.

To defeat an enemy, you must first understand the enemy. You must entice the other person to open up, allowing you to get to the heart of the issue. This is a critical first step.

Ask open-ended "feeling" questions, or try a quick tactic such as:

> "On a scale of 1 to 10, what is your confidence level with this decision?"
>
> Then follow up with "What part is keeping you from making it a 10?"

Once you've identified the objection, don't respond to the objection with a "but," but rather an "I agree" or "I understand." It diffuses them, and creates a dynamic where you are on their side, as opposed to you becoming an opponent. The great sales and motivational speaker Zig Ziglar once taught:

> "When an objection occurs, always use the fundamentals of FEEL, FELT, FOUND. It gives you an extra cushion of time and allows the prospect to identify with others." Such as: 'I see how you FEEL! Others have FELT the same way too until they FOUND...'"

This is similar to one of my favorite tongue-in-cheek overcoming objection tactics:

> **OBJECTION:** "It just seems like our payments are too high."
>
> **RESPONSE:** "Yeah, when I bought my first home, my payments were too high, too—but I got used to it. Besides, they wouldn't have approved you if they didn't think you could handle it, so sign right here and we're all set to go!"

Lines like this were so effective, they successfully triggered the U.S. credit and foreclosure crisis.

Overcoming objection tactics are great for the business world. But, of course, I've always wondered....

"Wouldn't it be great if...?"

Wouldn't it be great if I could utilize such overcoming objection tactics in the dating world? It would go something like this:

OBJECTION: *"Sorry, I'm just really into my career right now."*

RESPONSE: *"I see how you feel. My last girlfriend was really into her career, too, until I came along and showed her some things in life are more important than work."*

OBJECTION: *"Sorry, you just live too far away, and I'm not interested in a long-distance relationship."*
RESPONSE: *"What if I move in with you, would that be close enough?"*

OBJECTION: *"Sorry, I'm already married."*

RESPONSE: *"Well, I certainly understand your hesitance. However, since the divorce rate is over 50%, can I give you my card to keep just in case?"*

OBJECTION: *"Can't we just be friends?"*
RESPONSE: *"Friends with benefits?"*

One of the most depressing days in a man's life is when a female actually objects with the words:

"Sorry, but you're just too old for me."

Uggghh... so depressing. Such a cold dose of reality!

But, I'm a positive thinker, and experienced in sales, so I thought I would be prepared with ways to overcome such objections to make younger females at least consider the possibilities. Some examples might include:

OBJECTION: *"Sorry, but you're just too old for me."*
RESPONSE: *"Oh, come on....I'm the type of guy your parents would love. After all, we went to high school together."*

OBJECTION: *"Sorry, but you're just too old for me."*

RESPONSE: *"Hmmm... OK. How about I give you my card and you can give me a call in 2 or 3 years when you turn 21?"*

OBJECTION: *"Sorry, but you're just too old for me."*

RESPONSE: *"You may think I'm too old, but I'm really immature for my age. I have a MySpace page and everything. Wanna go get some ice cream?"*

OK, I'm only joking on these... kind of. I'd consider adding the fact that *Hannah Montana* is my favorite show, but by then they would have already sought out the authorities.

Chapter 46

PERSISTENCE:
DON'T ACCEPT "NO"
FOR AN ANSWER
(THAT IS—UNTIL THEY GET A RESTRAINING ORDER)

Inspirational speaker Glenna Salsbury once presented a program for one of my organizations in Florida, in which she told a delightful story of how she and her husband met many years before. She was driving near the beach in California, about 20 miles from her home, when she came upon a stop sign. She struck eyes with this guy driving the opposite direction. He promptly made a U-turn, got behind her, and followed her all the way down the coast 20 miles to her home. They met, spoke, and were eventually married less than one year later.

Sitting next to her at the head table after the program, I said *"That was a great story on how your husband followed you home 20 years ago. Of course, nowadays we call that STALKING."*

She laughed. So, I continued...

"It was definitely an inspirational story though," I added. *"It gives great hope to stalkers everywhere. Perhaps they, too, can follow the woman of their dreams home and marry her someday."*

I've long dreamt of having women follow me or show up at my door, but the only women who follow me are female police officers, and the only women who show up at my door are wearing a Pizza Hut hat.

Nevertheless, while this method was successful for her husband, it's probably not the strategy you'd want to employ with that next hot driver you see on the road *(nor your next hot prospect)*. Cell phones and SWAT teams have become such a hindrance to romantic roadway courtships these days. Can't people just say *"No"* without getting the authorities involved?

As a customer, I'm actually not that good at saying *"No"* to salespeople at all. I know what salespeople go through, so it's difficult to flatly reject someone who is trying hard to make a living. In fact, I often respect and surrender to honest, old-fashioned persistence, no matter what job in sales they have. Advertising reps, printing reps, ice-cream samplers at the grocery store, you name it.

However, sometimes these well-trained salespeople just take persistence a bit too far. They come to my front door and keep badgering and badgering, overcoming every objection before badgering some more. *"But, Mr. Masters how about this,"* and *"Mr. Masters how about that,"* and *"Mr. Masters what if we include this"*… until finally I simply reach the BREAKING POINT and say *"ALRIGHT, ALRIGHT—JUST GIVE ME TWO DOZEN BOXES OF THIN MINTS—NOW GET THE HELL OUT OF HERE ALREADY!!!"*

OK, I'm just kidding on that. I love the Girl Scouts.

I especially love the ones who sell their own cookies, rather than having their parents hawk stuff cubicle-to-cubicle at work using high-pressure obligation tactics. **Nevertheless, sometimes it takes persistence to get what you really want in life, and it feels that much better when you finally get it.**

Chapter 47

BUYING THEM A FEW DRINKS
NEVER HURT

It's worthy to outline a cardinal rule of etiquette when dining with a client... or a first date. **Ask the other person if they would like an alcoholic beverage first, before you order one.** If they say "Yes," it is OK for you to have one, as well. If they say "No," then you should not.

Naturally, the only time I didn't pay attention to that rule, I got burned. I had just begun a first date, when the waiter wrongfully turned to me first and asked if I wanted a drink. Preoccupied with the surroundings and remembering whether I brought my first date cheat sheet, I went ahead and ordered my standard first date drink first. Then, he turned to my date for her order when she responded, "No, thanks. I just got out of rehab yesterday." Yikes!

So, I quickly turned to the waiter and said "Is it too late to change my order to chocolate milk?" Then, amusing myself, I added "I'd still like to have the umbrella and whipped cream, though."

That's OK. I didn't like her anyway. She looked like Woody Harrelson.

On yet another occasion, I had a first date with a woman who apparently tried to impress men by how much alcohol she could handle. Granted, back in my fraternity days that was a MAJOR turn-on, but now that I was in the professional world, visions of a future mate dancing half-naked on tables at the company holiday party was not.

I drank two sips of my first beer and wasn't even past the top label, when she was already waving the waiter over for

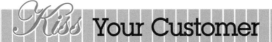

round two. I started questioning my manhood. To this day, I've never seen a person drink that fast who wasn't competing in a collegiate beer-chugging contest. I knew I was in trouble when I began telling the waiter, *"One for me, three for her."*

How about a strategy of buying drinks for potential clients so they will tell you what they *really think* about your company and services? That's exactly what a marketing agency did back in 1999. Marketers were starving for *"real scoop"* from their focus group, so they invited young professional women to sit with their friends and chat about financial services, while enjoying wine and cocktails all evening. That's right, they intentionally got these women a little *"liquored up,"* so they would *"open up"* about their honest feelings on the industry. I wonder if the facilitator was a hard-up single guy just looking to give one of them a ride home...

When I was in management, I ran into an old buddy of mine who worked in sales for a major shipping company. My company shipped a high volume of products to our clients, and he really wanted a piece of our account. He tried to schmooze me with baseball tickets, golf outings, happy hours, etc. Finally, through a process of meetings during the year, we decided to give his company a shot.

Little did he know that deep down I had very little loyalty to him. What kind of a manager would I be if I sacrificed quality and service to our clients in exchange for a few drinks and baseball tickets? If his company screwed up, it would be over. If his company performed well, we'd stay. The perks were just an inconsequential sidebar.

You get what you ask for in life—with clients, dates, and friends. If you try to use people through buying them a few drinks and showing them a good time, you just might end up with someone using you for a few free drinks and a good time.

Relationships built on shallow terms will be shallow and short-lived. Relationships based on sincerity will be sincere and sustaining.

Chapter 48

IF ALL ELSE FAILS, BEG!

There's something to be said for sympathy and pity in this world. Sometimes, it works. In fact, I think all men have mastered the *"don't you feel sorry for me"* puppy dog look by age 25.

I tried to perfect the puppy dog look for over 30 years, but women just weren't responding to my drool and foaming at the mouth.

I now understand women prefer games of cat and mouse instead.

Perpetually intrigued by this topic, I've playfully asked female members of my audience: *"How many women have ever gone out with a guy... just because you felt SORRY for them!?!?"*

Amazingly, almost HALF of women raise their hands to this question *(where were these women when I was in high school?)*

Of course, I then turn to the gentlemen in the audience and say, *"For all those single guys who might be desperate or down on your luck right now... Look at all the women who just raised their hand. See—you've got a chance!"*

I love bringing hope and inspiration to people.

Indeed, my experience capitalizing on sympathy and pity began in high school. I was such a skinny dork I did bicep curls with two cheerios taped to the ends of a toothpick.

My lone high school girlfriend actually admitted the only reason she dated me is because I was so pathetic she felt sorry for me.

"Hey, whatever works!"

Since then, I've done everything I could to gain weight. Pumping iron, drinking protein shakes, eating that 3rd dessert late at night... so, pity me no more. I'm actually working on a GUT now—how exciting!

This sympathy concept can easily be translated into the sales world, as well. I once managed a salesperson who overtly displayed many photos of his wife and 3 children on his desk, in clear view of potential customers. His closing line would actually be *"Here's a picture of my wife, Karen, and my 3 boys, Justin, Daniel, and Jacob. Now, you can go ahead and help me feed them this month by signing right here. We all thank you so much."*

Again, whatever works.

Soon I learned it is common practice for salespeople everywhere to openly display family photos on their office desk. It humanizes a salesperson. **After all, salespeople are people, too.** Not a bad idea.

If you don't have your own spouse and kids yet, any picture of a family will do. In fact, just leave in the model portraits that already come inside the frame—that will work just fine.

Lastly, have you ever seen a salesperson so bad, you felt sorry enough for them that you bought whatever they were selling? I think we've all donated to such a cause before. Did you know Leadpile.com actually sponsored a *"World's Worst Salesperson"* contest on YouTube? Wow. Have fun proudly listing that award on your next resumé.

Impressive!

Chapter 49

SOMETIMES
IT'S BETTER TO BE
LUCKY THAN GOOD

I used to be so unlucky.

I would never catch the elevator before it closed. Traffic cops shut down my exit on my way to work. I would never get the attractive waitresses.

I would always miss her by just ONE lousy table, and would glare over into her section as my homely waitress approached.

ME: *"Can I move over into THAT section?"*

WAITRESS: *"Oh, sorry... but that section is smoking."*

ME: *"Yeah, smoking HOT!"*

Fortunately, I'm much luckier now. Well, sort of.

I get seated with the attractive waiters.

With all sincerity... I AM a lucky person now. I really am.

I catch foul balls at baseball games. I always seem to win door prizes and raffles. I find money on the ground *(that wasn't just dropped by a little old lady)*. Out of 137 airplane seats, my hockey hero Mario Lemieux and his wife stroll down the aisle and sit next to me. I drive on Highway 95, and live to tell about it.

I always feel like I get lucky breaks in life. Whenever I make a big decision or take a risk, things always seem to work out.

I AM lucky. It's a GREAT feeling to be lucky!!

I need to start buying more lottery tickets.

So, then I stop and think: ***"What makes me a lucky person? When did this transformation happen? And, how?"***

After contemplating, there really wasn't an exact moment. However, I do remember simply beginning to tell people I was lucky whenever something good might happen.

> **GIRL:** *"Ohmygosh... Congratulations!"*
> **ME:** *"Thanks. I'm lucky. I'm a lucky person."*

I actually think I began saying it just to impress women. I was smart enough to understand that saying *"I'm a lucky person"* was much more sexy to a woman than looking down at the ground grumbling:

> **GUY:** *"I'm so unlucky... nothing good ever happens to me."*
> **GIRL:** *"Gee—let's go out again sometime. You're a barrel of laughs!!"*

So, I kept saying it. Then, I started believing it. The more I said it and the more I believed it, the more lucky things would happen to me.

> *"I know for sure that what we dwell on is who we become."*
> *– Oprah Winfrey*

I believe with all of my heart that luck is a self-fulfilling prophecy, in business and in life.

Not only do we create our own luck, but we attract luck through our constant thoughts, feelings, and attitude. For better or for worse, we are all a current realization of our prior self-fulfilling prophecies.

"I am the greatest. I said that even before I knew I was."
– Muhammad Ali

Luck can be relative, based on one's attitude in a given situation.

One of my early mentors, Author/Speaker James Malinchak, once shared this business parable:

Two salespeople with rival shoe companies boarded a plane for a remote third world country. Upon arrival, both looked around and saw that none of the people in this country wore shoes at all.

The first salesperson jumped on the phone to his headquarters and exclaimed: *"Get me on the first plane outta here. This is RIDICULOUS. Nobody even wears shoes in this country!"*

The second salesperson jumped on the phone to his headquarters and exclaimed: *"Ship me as many cases of shoes as fast as you possibly can. It's a gold mine here."*

Some guys get all the luck.

Chapter 50

Closing means getting the date, or getting the sale.
Closing means getting commitment on any desired outcome.
Closing means getting the other person to say "Yes."

As with a business proposal or a marriage proposal—the greater the relationship that is established, the greater the chance the other person will say "Yes."

Man:	*"Will you marry me?"*
Woman:	*"What's your name again?"*

We must build a bond, and build a trust strong enough between ourselves and the other person, that closing is easy.

So, what does it take to be a great closer?

Are you smooth? Are you experienced? Do you have techniques that work for you almost every time?

Several of my favorite closing tactics are the *"Either/Or"* close, the *"If I could, would you"* close, and the *"Assumptive"* close. For legal purposes, I recommend any of these over the ever-popular *"bait and switch"* close.

With the *"Either/Or"* close, we change a *"Yes-No"* decision to *"Yes-Yes"* by asking which of two options work best, such as:

"Which would work best for you, the leather recliner or the cloth recliner?"

"Would you like me to send over one of my contracts, or is there a standard contract on your end you normally use?"

"Would you prefer the expensive model, or the second most expensive model?"

This is also a classic format when securing a sales appointment:

"Do you prefer a weekend or weekday? Great, morning or afternoon? Great, I've got either a 2:00 or 4:00 available, which works best for you?"

Examples of the *"Either/Or"* method in the dating world could include:

"So, your place or mine?" (Does anyone actually use this?)

"So, do you prefer Asian or Italian?" (That's restaurants, not women.)

With the *"If I could, would you"* close, we try to find a missing link that would entice the prospect to commit first, which is something we already know we can accommodate.

"If I could throw in the extended warranty, would you buy today?"

"If I could get tickets to John Mayer, would you go with me?"

This method also lessens the risk for rejection. The other person isn't saying "No," they are saying "No" to a hypothetical situation. Besides, you don't want to be stuck with two $125 tickets to John Mayer if she's going to say "No."

Of course, if she does say "No," she's basically saying she's not willing to go out with you even if you bribe her with John Mayer tickets. That's pretty bad.

With the "Assumptive" close, we ask a question which essentially passes over the closing question, with the assumption that the buying decision is already a foregone conclusion.

"So, what's the first piece of furniture you're going to buy for your new home?"

"So, what do you want to name our kids someday?"

Another key to closing is the ability to create a sense of urgency.

It's human nature to wait, and to not make a decision. Every consumer wants to wait for the perfect time to commit. A perfect time that usually never comes. Examples of consumers stalling include "I'll think about it," "I'll sleep on it," or "maybe after Christmas."

There always must be a reason to commit NOW, as opposed to waiting.

"Mortgage rates will never be lower."

"This product will be discontinued tomorrow."

"I could be engaged by this time next week."

Lastly, it's also important to understand the best lingo to use, and how to use it wisely. Sales guru Tom Hopkins identified that *"No one likes to buy, but people love to own."* The word *"buying"* means spending money, which has a negative connotation. The word *"owning"* means enjoying, which has a positive connotation.

Never ask a prospect: *"Wouldn't you love to buy this?"* Instead ask: *"Wouldn't you love to own this?"*

Indeed, all of these closing lines work much more effectively than some of these... well... not-so-good closing lines:

"Please, I need one more sale to make my quota... and my rent."

"Trust me, sir, chicks DIG 9-foot speakers. Now sign here."

"Gimme that credit card or I'll beat your head in."

Chapter 51

OVERCOME BUYER'S REMORSE

Have you ever woken up and felt so regretful... so remorseful... so guilty after a night of indulgence? You can't believe you had such a total lack of self-discipline, as you surrendered to temptation and impulse.

Your poor judgment succumbed to a good-looking, smooth talker for something new and exciting—but when you woke up the next morning, you came to your senses and said *"Why in the world did I do that... What was I thinking?!?!?"*

So, you grabbed your receipt and took that big screen plasma TV right back to the store.

You know that scenario, right?

Sometimes the sale doesn't end at the sale. Whether it's a customer return the day after an impulse purchase, or a 72-hour *"right of recension"* law many states have on big-ticket items. If people are unhappy, they can change their minds. Or, they might accept that purchase, but not make a similar purchase from the same company or salesperson in the future.

Similarly, many states even have a 3-day waiting period for marriage licenses to take effect as well. I suppose that's for brides who either REALLY didn't enjoy their wedding night, or finally sobered up from their drive-thru wedding in Las Vegas.

People who are being propositioned in either sales or relationships have the same fears:

☹ People don't want to get burned.

☹ People don't want to fall for something.

☹ People don't want to get taken advantage of.

☹ People don't want to be made to look stupid.

☹ People don't want to be pictured as "Sucker of the Month," proudly displayed in the employee lounge.

It's amazing how some wishy-washy customers attempt to find ways to wiggle out of a deal sometimes. Like slimy little worms trying to escape from a live bait bucket.

Don't let 'em escape! Get 'em hooked for good.

When I first began as a sales manager, I worked closely with my general manager and longtime friend Rick. Rick taught me how important it was to always congratulate new clients immediately after a contract was signed. Rick and I would both enjoy making the customer feel as if they just won, and got the customer EXCITED about their decision.

"Congratulations! Who are you going to call first?"
"Many people have made the same decision, and they couldn't be happier!"
"We're going to go bankrupt if we keep selling to customers like you!"

Rick and I always wanted to make the other person feel good about what just happened, so they would return again... with others. We wanted that person to jump on the phone and tell friends and colleagues what a great deal they just landed, and that others should take advantage, too.

Call the other person the following morning to ensure the excitement level is still high. Make the other person feel confident of their decision by reinforcing the positives. Ask if they have any questions, or if there is anything you can do for them.

Don't just say *"Sayonara."*

Failing to call the following morning will only foster paranoia, and escalate feelings of remorse... about anything they might be remorseful about.

KEEP YOUR CUSTOMER
SATISFIED

Important in business. **Very** important in relationships.
You get the point.

DON'T
TAKE THE OTHER PERSON FOR GRANTED

I'd like to think this book is just as much about how to improve our personal relationships through applying business principles, as it is vice-versa.

Have you ever had a day when you treated your client better than you treated your significant other when you arrived home?

Consider the difference in reaction after someone might spill a drink on new carpet, both at the office and at home:

To Client: *"Don't worry about it, Bob—no sense in crying over spilled milk. That should come right up. So, tell me more about your trip to Idaho again."*

To Loved One: *"Damn it, Chris—Watch what you are doing!"*

So, why does this happen? What exactly is the logic?

Your Customer

"Well, I'm paid to be nice at work."

"I had to be patient with people all day. Thank God that's over with!"

"I had a rough day today, so I needed to take it out on someone."

Really? You needed to take it out on someone? That must be your favorite tip from the book Marriage Etiquette by Ike Turner.

Sometimes we need to remember to make our loved ones feel as special as we do our clients. We should remind the other person how we feel about them. Call for no reason. Send them a playful 10-second text... anytime. Leave them a surprise note in an unlikely place.

One Spring afternoon, I learned my girlfriend at the time had scheduled a tanning appointment for 3:45. I raced ahead to arrive by 3:30, and handed the lone employee an envelope with a note to hand her upon arrival. "It's important!"

The note read:

"WOW... would I love to be YOUR tanning bed for 30 minutes."

I tried to sneak into her tanning bed early to enhance the surprise, but someone was still in there.

"Sorry, dude!"

Oops. Got burned on that one.

Besides small touches in life, what can you truly help the other person with? This could be providing help with a hobby, running weekend errands, or even applying your business talents to help the other person in their job.

In relationships, I've always tried to help the person I was dating in their professional life. When I dated a sales professional, I'd give her clients, resources, or even just basic sales advice. I didn't even ask for commission with most of them.

What's important is, in either business or relationships, taking the other person for granted leads to complacency, and complacency is the enemy. Complacency can lull us into a false sense of security.

152

In this busy world, we shouldn't take our loved ones for granted: *"Oh, she will always be there for me. She loves me!"*

In this busy world, we shouldn't take our best clients for granted: *"Oh, she will always be there for us. She loves us!"*

We must be cognizant that we are in constant competition with *"the other guy,"* who is always trying to swoop in and win over our clients' hearts. This threat is real. And, understanding how real this threat is will cause us to be on alert, helping squelch complacency.

It will also help us realize how much we truly appreciate our client, and how much we shouldn't take that relationship for granted. The more the other person feels appreciated on a continual basis, the less likely they are to go astray, tempted by *"the other guy."*

Hmmm... maybe this isn't so different from our loving relationships, either.

Chapter 54

Gentlemen: *When was the last time you bought a dozen roses for your significant other... when it wasn't Valentine's Day?*

To clarify, when was the last time you bought a dozen roses for your significant other when it wasn't Valentine's Day—AND, there wasn't a card attached which read *"I'm sorry, Dear. It will never happen again!"*

My good friend Steve once sent a dozen roses to his girlfriend, attached with a card which read *"Just because..."*

Two days later, she sent a dozen roses to his office, attached with a card which read *"Because why?"*

Cute.

Although, their conversations might become a bit expensive after a few months (*isn't text messaging just a little cheaper?*)

My longtime friend Matt once creatively transformed a pack of "Bubblicious" gum into "Babe-a-licious" gum for his girlfriend. The re-designed packaging was complete with ingredients such as *"smart, funny, cool, caring, and pretty,"* and was produced by the "Christine Bubble Gum Company."

I tried that concept once using "Boob-a-licious" gum, but it didn't work quite as well.

My close friend Dave, I must say, is the master of creating clever gift experiences for everyone in his life.

Dave has bobble heads custom-made in the image of the other person. Dave superimposes photos of the other person with celebrities or exotic backgrounds. Dave comically rewrites lyrics from TV theme songs and Elvis hits, and performs at celebrations. Dave has never settled for a *"normal"* gift in his life.

Indeed, the words *"let's just stop by Target"* aren't in Dave's vocabulary (unless it's for those TASTY cherry Icees from the food bar.)

I remember when Dave and I used to work together. I would always brainstorm new creative surprises for a client or girlfriend, just trying to impress him. I'd finally mastermind a fantastic idea, and storm into his office like an excited kindergartner running home to show Dad his new drawing from school.

ANDY: *"So, what do you think about THAT?!?!"*

DAVE: *"That's great, Andy. This year will be the 20th year in a row I do that for my cousin Jeff on his birthday."*

ANDY: *"Oh."*

Dave relishes creating memorable experiences for others. He truly makes the special moments in people's lives special. It has helped define his character to many. He and his brother even created a line of imaginative greeting cards sold across the country, to compete with the lame and predictable cards most of us have to choose from.

"Happy Girth-day!" said the elephant.

Please.

Lastly, of course, such special tokens of appreciation in life always work great for clients.

So, when was the last time you gave one of your best clients a gift for no reason, when it wasn't the holidays?

If you're in manufacturing, surprise your client with a creative cake. Have their logo drawn with icing, and spell out a message on the cake with cute little bolts. Something like *"Mr. Blotschke, thanks again for your orders of aluminum piping."*

Just make sure the bolts are edible.

Being creative, thoughtful, and clever is FUN. You will look forward to that next client meeting. You will look forward to that next birthday party. You will look forward to that next wedding... reception.

Making the other person feel special will totally make your day.

Chapter 55

UNDERSTAND THEIR WANTS and NEEDS

Millions of books have been written on understanding the wants and needs of the customer. Millions of books have also been written on understanding the wants and needs of the opposite sex. A couple of my personal favorites in the relationship world include:

Men Are From Mars, Women Are From Venus, written by Dr. John Gray. Nice, but I would have opted for *Women Are From Mars, Men Are From Earth*.

Everything Men Know About Women, "written" by Cindy Cashman. The book is 128 blank pages. I think she's giving us too much credit.

So, what do we really know about our customers? Why do our customers buy? Why do our customers not buy? What makes our customers happy? What do our customers really want?

Too often, we just assume. We give them price, and they really want service. We give them service, and they really want price. **It is imperative we uncover what our customers really think.**

Do we survey them?

Do we conduct focus groups?

Do we encourage comments and feedback?

Do we tap their phone lines?

Do we hire secret shoppers to befriend them and elicit the real inside scoop?

Kiss Your Customer

Do we really get to know our customer, and truly engage our customer on a personal and professional level to understand what they really want?

In other words, we have to ask. We can't read their minds.

We should be observant, elicit information, collect data, and utilize the data.

Perhaps the most critical step in that process is actually utilizing the data. People appreciate when we ask about their wants and needs. People are blown away when we actually apply it.

Even with the smallest pieces of information.

A good friend of mine from Dallas, named Richard, frequently travels to Cape Girardeau, Missouri, on business. One afternoon, the front desk clerk at the Holiday Inn Express noticed that Richard would always pick a strawberry Jolly Rancher out of the basket at the counter.

She logged that tidbit, and stored it in his customer profile. However, it didn't stop there. From that point on, 4-5 strawberry Jolly Ranchers were placed on his nightstand before he arrived.

And that's without sneaking 17 cents onto his bill.

Richard's not a CEO or a celebrity, either.

But it sure makes him feel like one.

Richard doesn't spend time surfing 500 travel websites to book a room in Cape Girardeau, Missouri, anymore. He keeps the manager's card in his wallet, and simply calls the hotel front desk directly whenever he needs another reservation.

In a world of tight budgets, often the smallest gestures are what keep a customer coming back for more.

What if we possessed such a simple piece of data on every customer? How much loyalty could we foster if we actually used it? How powerful could that be?

In relationships, it is paramount to understand what the other person wants or needs. Among other things, it comes in handy for holiday gifts, birthday gifts, or just the occasional surprise. We could simply ask, but that ruins the surprise factor. It may also seem a bit lazy and uncreative.

"Just tell me what you want and I'll go buy it."

Again, we should be observant, elicit information, and utilize the data. **People give us clues every day.**

> *What is their favorite weekend getaway?*
> *What is their favorite hobby?*
> *What is their favorite sports team?*
> *What is their favorite spa?*
> *What is their favorite color of underwear?*

On that note, I know one guy who continued to buy his wife sexy lingerie each year for her birthday, even after she hinted that was really a gift for HIM, not her. To finally illustrate her point, she sarcastically gift-wrapped a pair of pink Winnie-the-Pooh underwear for his next birthday, complete with a matching pink Winnie-the-Pooh hat.

I can only imagine how adorable you look in those, Brock.

Chapter 56

DON'T BE A CHEAPSKATE

According to a poll by the University of Denver, the number one problem for couples in America is disagreements over money. It's also a pretty big issue between companies and their customers.

Being considered a cheapskate can be quite damaging, in either business or personal relationships. It can make someone look selfish, greedy, and unappreciative of the other party.

Earning a reputation of a cheapskate can develop any time, even at unofficial gatherings or business events. Don't be the person at the holiday party who happens to hover by the free appetizer table all night. Nobody likes a grazer, and nobody wants to see how many little smokies people can stuff in their pockets for later (*Additional info: I've found they don't taste as good later topped with lint sprinkles, anyway*).

Don't be cheap with holiday gifts. After an entire year of gross profit your clients have given you, at least spring for something of value, not to mention unique, personalized, and clever.

Every year our office supply vendors gave each of us managers one of those big popcorn tins. That's an ideal example of a present that's so big, it looks like it's not that cheap, but in reality they bought them for the "rollback the prices" cost of $4.97.

"Wow, another popcorn tin to put under the tree. Just what I asked Santa for in my letter to the North Pole!"

Cheap bastards. That'll be a regift.

Regifting is common practice among the cheapskate elite. For those amateur cheapskates, regifting is the process of receiving a gift that you don't want to keep (usually because it is CRAP), then re-wrapping it to give to some other sorry sap. It's the Christmas version of hot potato. An American holiday tradition.

What's even worse is regifting to a girlfriend—using a gift returned by an ex-girlfriend.

I only did that once.

What's the big deal if she never found out? Especially if the previous girlfriend only wore it once or twice, and the new girlfriend was the same size.

Besides, it just saved me another trip to Victoria's Secret. GREAT outfit!

Lastly, **the world of garage sales provides us an international list of best practices for all cheapskates to abide by.** It also provides us cheap entertainment. I think the Comedy Channel should host an annual event at the world's biggest garage and call it the *"World Cheapskate Championships."*

I'll never forget when I helped a friend organize a garage sale before she moved. She kept haggling back and forth with someone over this ugly candle.

> *"How much for the candle?"*
> *"50 cents."*
> *"I'll give you a quarter."*
> *"50 cents."*
> *"I'll give you a QUARTER."*
> *"FIFTY CENTS."*
> *"30 cents... TOPS."*
> *"Look, 50 CENTS—or GET THE HELL OUT OF MY DRIVEWAY!"*
> *"You know what... YOU CAN KEEP YOUR DAMN CANDLE."*

And that was her Aunt.

Unreal.

Just save your time, donate your stuff to a good cause, and take the tax write-off... please.

With all of these examples, I do understand that everyone has a budget—both personal and professional. But, you have to make wise decisions on where to cut corners and where not to. Be a cheapskate with everything else, so you can afford to be generous when you need to. This includes the most important clients in your life, and the most important people in your life.

People love to feel valued. People love to feel pampered. People love getting stuff for free.

Except popcorn tins.

Chapter 57

The unwritten rules for who should pick up the tab at a restaurant are:

> *Salespeople should pay for clients.*
>
> *Men should pay for women.*
>
> *Colleagues should split the bill.*
>
> *Rich people should pay for everyone.*
>
> *Children over the age of 3 should fend for themselves.*

Depending on the estimate and industry, it costs 4-7 times the amount of money to find a new customer than it does to retain a current customer. It also costs money to find a new relationship.

Cover charges, online dating services, trendy clothes, gym memberships, and liposuction procedures aren't cheap.

With either business or dating, we spend (invest) money up front during the "impression" stage, allowing us to spend less later during the "relationship" stage *(also refer to Chapter 65: Get Them To Fall in Love With You And You Can Get Away With Almost Anything)*.

When on a first date, I've always insisted on paying. Perhaps it's just the gentlemanly Midwesterner in me. However, it is a nice gesture if my date at least reaches into her pocketbook for the token *"Oh, let me at least pay for my half."*

I only took someone up on that once. It was a REALLY bad date.

Have you ever heard of those guys who have women take them out to dinner, and pay? I had one friend after college who didn't even have a car, and kept finding women to pick him up and take him on dates everywhere. Are you kidding me?

Must be nice to have the nickname *"Sugar Mama Shawn."*

Then there are the guys who discreetly try to pay for dinner by sneaking a 20% off coupon, restaurant gift card, or some other type of *"free"* promotional offer.

"SURE—I've got this. Don't worry about it... it's on me!"

Hey, I have to spend those McDonald's Monopoly winners somewhere.

Marvin Gardens, baby!!

In business, have you ever noticed when someone takes you out for a lunch meeting, your conscience tells you not to order the most expensive thing on the menu, but when you take clients out, they order the $75 Surf & Turf with two glasses of expensive wine?

So be it. It *is* an investment.

Some companies (or accountants within those companies), don't appreciate the concept of *"return on investment."* They are only fixated on *"return."*

As a grateful salesperson, I decided to purchase a more *"personalized"* holiday card for my client—to send in addition to the stale corporate card our company was already mailing each client. I signed the card, closed the envelope, and sent it down to the company mailroom to be stamped and mailed.

The following day, I received a phone call from our mailroom supervisor, who informed me that I now needed to provide my own stamp, or complete a *"reimbursement request form"* for the postage, which would probably be denied.

I said *"For 37 cents? For a holiday card to my client??"*

He said the Director of Accounting also told others the company wouldn't reimburse for holiday card postage beyond what was already paid for, and he was trying to be consistent.

I said, *"Yeah, a consistent SCHMUCK."*

And some companies wonder why their best salespeople always leave.

Costs associated with relationship building are an investment. Being too concerned with saving a few pennies up front can cost you big dollars later.

It's certainly important for companies to try to cut costs at every turn. That's sound business. However, as with government spending, businesses endure out-of-control waste at the rate of tens of thousands and even millions of dollars each year, often unnoticed and unaddressed. Attacking each of these cost-saving opportunities should be exhausted first. Cutting costs through being stingy with clients and employees should be considered last, if at all.

Clients and employees are the lifeblood of every company.

MANAGE EXPECTATIONS

"You told the client we'll do WHAT?

By WHEN??

For HOW MUCH???"

Salespeople have a tendency to tell customers anything they want to hear to get the sale. Service reps have a tendency to tell customers anything they want to hear to make them happy. Unfortunately, this can create unrealistic expectations, and put undue stress on everyone in the organization.

Have you ever committed to an unreasonable time frame, price, or special request with someone?

"Suuuurrreee, I can get that to you by tomorrow."

"Suuuurrreee, I can slide you a 70% discount."

"Suuuurrreee, I can fly you to Paris for a date sometime."

So, why do we do this? Why do we cave in and tell people what they want to hear, instead of what they need to hear?

It's called conflict avoidance.

It should be called conflict procrastination.

Consider these two scenarios:

Let's say you were so busy on a given Friday, you were forced to skip lunch, and are starving by dinner. You meet three friends at a restaurant at 6:30, and the parking lot is full—with a crowd hovering outside the door.

"GREAT... this place is packed. I'm NEVER going to eat!"

You rush in and approach a 17-year old hostess, and ask in a frustrated voice *"How long is the wait?"*

In scenario one, a poorly trained hostess doesn't want to upset you, so she nervously responds *"About 10 minutes."*

In scenario two, a well-trained hostess responds *"Just to be up-front, we are quite busy this evening, so it could be up to a 30 minute wait."*

In either scenario, you consider that by the time you went somewhere else, parked, and waited, you might as well stick it out here.

So, you wait. After 20 minutes, your buzzer buzzes, and your table is ready.

In scenario one, when the hostess told you 10 minutes, your response is *"It's about time. She told me TEN MINUTES. I hate this place!"*

In scenario two, when the hostess told you 30 minutes, your response is *"Awesome... my buzzer is buzzing already. Food, here I come! I love this place!"*

Don't paint yourself into a corner by over-committing to promises you may not be able to fulfill. Put yourself and your team members in position to succeed, not fail. Put yourself and your team members in position to be a hero to others, not a goat.

Exercise the customer satisfaction and stress relief principle: ***"Under-promise and over-deliver."***

When we're placed under pressure from co-workers, clients, friends, or even strangers, each day we should be armed with managing expectation phrases such as:

"Just to be up-front..."
"Just to give you a heads-up..."
"Hey, just hold on to your britches there, pal."

Importantly, I've emphasized a concept in my programs that we must manage expectations with ourselves. Yep. We need to "*under-promise and over-deliver*" in our own lives.

Too often we are victims of taking on too much, and "*spreading ourselves too thin.*" Coaching that third team. Serving on that fourth committee. Unrealistically trying to jam 17 things onto our "To-Do" list. Rushing to our pedicure appointment right before it closes.

We try too hard to be superheroes in every phase of our lives, every day. I term this "*Superhero Syndrome.*"

The vast majority of stress in life is completely self-inflicted.

Life is complicated enough. We should slow down. We should simplify. We should prioritize and focus our valuable time on our most important responsibilities, clients, and loved ones. This will create improvement in these areas, and create more time to enjoy life.

Setting realistic expectations can be applied to all phases of life. For instance, if you ever have a funny joke to tell, don't tell everyone it's a funny joke before you tell it, or it won't be as funny.

I remember friends telling me how unbelievably hilarious the 2007 movie *SuperBad* was, and that I HAD to go see it right away. After such build-up and expectation, I finally saw *Super-Bad*, and thought it was just... well... super bad.

Trust me, *The 40-Year-Old Virgin* it was not.

In dating, it's always nice to get a referral or positive recommendation from a friend, but I've always hated when someone went way overboard by ranting and raving about this AWESOME, FUNNY, SMART, ATHLETIC, GREAT LOOKING guy. OK, maybe I didn't mind that much. However, I definitely thought to myself:

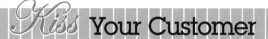

"GREAT... there's no WAY I can live up to THOSE expectations on a first date. THANKS A LOT. We've just set the other person up for total disappointment!"

Maybe we should tell all blind dates that we are ugly before we meet the other person, so they are happily surprised.

If they show up.

Of course, if they're blind, I suppose it doesn't matter.

Chapter 59

BE UP-FRONT FROM THE START!

Besides, as the other person, don't we just want to know? Don't we just want someone to provide us with realistic expectations? **Don't we just want someone to be up-front with us from the start?**

Sure we do.

This is certainly true with the beginning of relationships. People just want to know up front where the relationship is heading, and what the intentions of the other person really are.

"I'm on the rebound, just needing some companionship right now."

"I'm looking for some short-term fun until my next serious relationship pops up."

"My biological clock is ticking, and I want a baby. In like nine months from today."

We don't want to waste time, money, effort, and emotions if it's not necessary. As the other person, we just want to know. Straight up.

That reminds me of my favorite song by Laker girl Paula Abdul – *"Straight up, now tell me do ya really want to love me forever, or are you just having fun?"*

Hey, wait a second… didn't I cite this Paula song already?

With two references from Paula Abdul and none from Mahatma Gandhi, I'm beginning to wonder about the inspirational credibility of this book.

I also considered adding another favorite Paula hit, *Opposites Attract*, as one of the 77 principles of this book. Great principle, though I'm sure Paula's replacement on *American Idol*, Ellen Degeneres, would disagree.

Nevertheless, as a customer, I just want to know what's going on (*unless it's what's really going on in a kitchen*). As a frequent traveler experienced in coping with airline shenanigans, I wish pilots and flight attendants would be more up front about flight status with its passengers. Why is this flight taking so long? Why is there so much turbulence? Why are we still circling around instead of landing?

Flight attendants should take charge and address the cabin, like Julie Hagerty's character in the 1980 classic, *Airplane*. After trying to calm anxious passengers during a troubling situation, she followed by asking:

> *"By the way, is there anyone on board*
> *who knows how to fly a plane?"*

As an interviewer, I would have loved to force candidates to be more up front and honest on resumés, instead of overstating past accomplishments and future promises. **Each candidate should be required to list a more accurate assessment of their past, and provide a more realistic expectation of future performance as a disclaimer on the back of each resumé.**

If so, many would read something like this:

- ☺ Job titles listed were really my boss's titles.
- ☺ I didn't quit my last three jobs, but was fired.
- ☺ Qualities listed as my strengths are really my weaknesses.
- ☺ The claim *"reached my quota"* actually meant *"reached our quota."* Like, as a team. That I rooted for.
- ☺ I am lazy. I take long lunches. I do the bare minimum to get by.
- ☺ I don't work well with others. I take credit for other people's work. I point fingers. I pass the buck.
- ☺ I embellish expense reports. I use company resources for personal projects. I've been known to steal office supplies. And an occasional small kitchen appliance from the employee break room.

Chapter 60

SOMETIMES "GOOD" JUST ISN'T GOOD ENOUGH

(WE MUST BE AWESOME!)

Ideally, we want each customer to enjoy our offerings so much, and exceed expectations so greatly, their reaction is similar to Meg Ryan's in *When Harry Met Sally*.

We want others to quip: *"I'll have what she's having."*

We want our customers to LOVE our company SO MUCH, they feel compelled to run out and TATTOO OUR LOGO ACROSS THEIR CHEST!

Such as the loyalty Harley Davidson has achieved. (This gives new meaning to the term *"corporate branding,"* by the way.)

I cannot WAIT for waves of my passionate fans to plaster their bodies with *KISS Your Customer* tattoos. Ladies, please email pics to andy@andy-masters.com.

Mom... feel free to get the ball rolling.

Loyalty isn't achieved by being average. Loyalty is achieved by being AWESOME.

I once presented a program in the small city of Greenwood, South Carolina. I don't recall the hotel I stayed in, for better or for worse. I was re-booked to present in Greenwood the following year, and made reservations at a different hotel, called *"The Inn on the Square."*

Technically, it was part of the Clarion hotel chain, but it had a very independent, non-corporate feel. It was small, but beautiful. Quaint, if you will. It spoke of southern hospitality, and was perfectly manicured with pride. The polite front desk clerk was reciting the standard info during check-in, and mentioned there would be complimentary breakfast between 7 – 10 a.m.

Sure. Many hotels have that.

Until she said it was made to order. Anything I wanted.

"Ummm... excuse me?"

No menu. No spread of yogurt and boxed cereal on the counter. No self-service "burn-at-your-own-risk" toaster. No pieces of stale bread sitting next to a fly swatter.

Just tell 'em what you want, and they'll retreat to the kitchen to whip up a southern-sized helping.

This wasn't an elite bed-&-breakfast resort, either. This was an under-a-$100 per night small town hotel (*with delightful lobby flowers, by the way*).

I didn't remember the hotel where the experience was just good. But I will *always* remember the hotel where the experience was AWESOME.

"The Inn on the Square."

What's amazing is this: How much more time and money did it take to provide such an AWESOME experience?

Another similar example was at a lodge where I was presenting in Branson, Missouri. At check-in, the front desk clerk mentioned that I would receive complimentary milk and cookies each night, and asked what time would I like them delivered to my room.

Really? Yummy!!

This is in contrast to *"nice"* expensive hotels that shuffle you in and out like cattle for $300+ per night, and have a tag on the bottled water in your room which reads *"This bottle of water is provided as a service to you for $4.95."*

Gee. Thanks.

This is on top of charging you $12.95 for wireless internet access, and $14.95 for two eggs and a slice of toast, plus a room service charge, plus hotel taxes, and plus 21% gratuity... that the bellhop somehow forgets to mention is already on the bill.

In dating, many idealistic romantic dreamers wait for *"The One." "My Soul Mate." "Mr. Right." "The One To Tattoo On My Chest."*

Many candidates come and go through years of dating, who might be good, but are simply not *"The One."*

Everyone is looking for *"The One,"* in either relationships, or whatever we seek in life or business. When we find average, we keep passing by. When we find AWESOME, we stop in our tracks.

Go by this rule of thumb: *"If it's not AWESOME, it sucks."*

This goes for your courtship, your product, your service, your presentations, your business cards, the presents you give, etc...

Anybody can be just OK.

Anybody.

Chapter 61

THE CUSTOMER Is ALWAYS RIGHT (EVEN WHEN THEY ARE WRONG)

Have you ever noticed that when a man has an argument with a woman, even if he wins, he really doesn't win?

I hate that.

The same holds true over arguments with customers.

Most of us possess a competitive streak to WIN, especially all arguments in which we truly believe we are right. NOTHING is more important than TRUTH and JUSTICE.

However, at times our passion to be right must submit to our passion to please. Please our customer. Please our significant other.

So, how much do you truly value your customer? What are you willing to sacrifice, or what are you willing to take, to keep each relationship? What are you willing to sacrifice, or what are you willing to take, to keep a customers' business?

I have a perfect illustration of this concept from one of my Mexico trips with a girlfriend and another couple.

One evening, the four of us ventured into a local bar/restaurant in a town near our resort. Trying to act authentic and experience Mexican culture, we promptly ordered a plate of nachos and four Coronas.

Extra cheese and salsa... Yummy!

However, while standing at the bar, I embarrassingly fumbled my attempt to look cool trying the *"insert the lime and flip the bottle"* technique. My Corona began fizzing uncontrollably like a VOLCANO about to ERUPT. I encountered a split-second bout of terror as this shaken bottle of Corona was about to EXPLODE… so I took TWO STEPS BACK, blindly LAUNCHED IT to the side, and KER-SPLASH!!!!

Right into the face of the 250-pound Mexican bouncer.

He was not amused.

"OHMYGOSH…..I am so sorry, Señor….Ohmygosh," I said in a whimpering please-don't-kill-me voice.

"Por Favor…POR FAVOR!!"

After a barrage of Spanish cursing which I'm sure equated to *"you stupid American tourist,"* he was leaning towards sparing my life as he knew the bar owner saw the entire incident behind us.

Fortunately for my sake (*and the sake of any future children I was planning on having*), the bar owner stepped in and explained to me in a Spanish accent:

"It is no problem, Señor. Americans explode Coronas all the time around here."

(Which, was basically saying, *"you stupid American tourist,"* just a bit more diplomatically.)

"I will go ahead and bring you another Corona, Señor. But I might ask that your female friend insert the lime for you this time," he said as he chuckled and patted me on my shoulder.

Thanks. I'm feeling really manly now.

After a moment, I began to realize how valued American tourists were to this business, and what they were willing to take. I looked deep into the eyes of this bar owner as he walked behind the counter. **It was then I understood that my business was his life. It was food for his sons and daughters. It was a way of life for every employee who depended on him.**

He was willing to sacrifice anything, to take anything, no matter who was right or wrong. Each customer was so deeply important to him.

Then I thought to myself:

"Wow. If we only valued our customers so much."

So...

How much do you value your customer?

How much does it matter if your customer is in the wrong?

How many Corona ker-splashes would you take in the face for your customer?

Chapter 62

AVOID DISSATISFACTION AT ALL COSTS

Upset customers can possess many different ways of expressing discontent. This may include asking to speak with a manager, filling out a comment card, or perhaps a subtle flipping of the bird.

Hey, learning there's no AARP discount can be quite upsetting.

Of course, the worst types of customers are those who do nothing. They don't tell you what's wrong, they just don't come back.

No chance to apologize or make it up to them.

I once took a date to this *"nice"* Italian restaurant, and all of our food was terribly underdone. I think the owner's name was Sal Monella.

Our entrée was overshadowed only by the service, which rivaled the best Driver's License Bureaus in the country. My date urged me to send the food back for a do-over, but I've always been hesitant of that option, given my fast-food work experience as a teenager.

"Oh, a COMPLAINER, huh? Yeah, I'll show him well-done!"

I'll happily opt for the check, and a stop-off at Taco Bell on the way home. I prefer Mexican to Italian, anyway.

I didn't say a word that evening, and needless to say, I haven't returned since.

However, just because customers may not say a word to you, that doesn't mean they're not saying a word.

"Ninety percent of the conversations about us happen when we're NOT in the room. The other ten percent are sugar coated."

– Andy Masters

It seems customer dissatisfaction is at an all-time high. Or, is that just perception? Has service become worse, or do customers simply have more ways, easier ways, and quicker ways to voice their discontent?

In the pre-Bill Gates era, upset customers had to commit to wasting valuable time picketing in front of an establishment, or telling each of their friends and family either in person, or using a phone. With a cord on it.

Thanks to email, social media, blogs, and the ability to text to your entire contact list all at once, it's never been easier for virtual venting to blast through customer cyberspace at frightening speed.

Needless to say, all such outlets can be particularly damaging with disgruntled ex's in the world of dating and relationships, too. Damage can include posting embarrassing information on Facebook and YouTube, or perhaps even selling an X-rated video to TMZ for millions of dollars—which I was a victim of once.

OK, I'm not quite that famous yet.

She only made thousands from TMZ. OK, hundreds from TMZ. OK, it got rejected from TMI (Too Much Information).

For further discussion of "disgruntled ex" dangers, please carefully read Chapter #69: *Create An Amicable Breakup (Never Burn Bridges)*.

Indeed, it has never been more dangerous and damaging to have a dissatisfied customer. In addition to email, texting, and social media, there are also more vendor review websites than ever, where within 2-3 clicks, any consumer can scroll through reviews of hotels and restaurants.

There's even a website for college students to rate their professor www.ratemyprofessor.com. Wow, that would have come in handy during college for researching which professors were hot—I mean, hard.

Discount airline JetBlue has gained much attention for its' use of the Internet and social media to engage customers, especially dissatisfied ones. Among other things, JetBlue has a staff whose only job is to surf social media and consumer websites to locate upset customers who feel wronged, and make it right.

Of course, then there's the really angry customer. This is the slightly disenchanted individual who simply can't find the right website on the Internet to vent their anger, so they create one on their own as a service to fellow disenchanted customers. That's right, the ever popular www.yourcompanysucks.com websites.

In fact, if you Google *"sucks.com,"* you will find such gems as www.Disney-sucks.com, www.Allstateinsurancesucks.com, and—taking it to the next level—www.Sprint-really-sucks.com.

That's OK. Any publicity is good publicity, right?

Eehhh...

Chapter 63

Perhaps it was too much pride, or just being stubborn, but I was never good at admitting my mistakes or saying I'm sorry when I was young. Then, I began working with **CUSTOMERS**, and began getting into **RELATIONSHIPS**.

I once dealt with this angry bald guy who was so upset with our service, he began cursing at me profusely, even calling my MOM names. I was hoping he was just experiencing a random bout of Tourette Syndrome. I think he was just upset because someone stole his Rogaine.

Fortunately, that Dairy Queen location has improved its service dramatically since then. However, at least our mistake was just confusing a Peanut Buster Parfait with a Banana Split.

There was once a hospital medical malpractice lawsuit against a hospital in Illinois, which experienced a slight surgical oversight. The doctor performed a vasectomy on some sorry sap instead of an appendectomy.

Ouch.

The patient sued the hospital for $40 million.

I'm guessing the *"I'm Sorry"* card the staff left on his hospital bed didn't quite cut it.

"It could be worse, sir. We could have confused you with the amputation procedure scheduled in the room next door with Dr. Bobbit."

So, when we do experience those little snafus in life, how do we *"make it up to them"*?

First, we have to let the other person vent, and empathize.

"I totally understand. I would be upset, as well, sir."

Ask what would make them happy in order to resolve the problem. If it's reasonable, see what you can do in a short period of time. If it's unreasonable, say *"I'm not sure if we can afford $40 million, but let me see what I can do to make you happy. Do you like ice cream?"*

In relationships, I've always found that women respond well to flowers, backrubs, or CASH.

One evening I did try to apologize by performing a midnight serenade, but it didn't work. Apparently, she just wasn't aroused by my rendition of *Welcome to the Jungle* by Guns 'N Roses.

Nor were her parents.

I KNEW I should have picked *Sweet Child of Mine*!

There have been conflicting opinions on the issue of apologies among the great thinkers in history. For instance:

> *"It takes a great deal of character strength to apologize quickly out of one's heart, rather than out of pity."*
> **– Stephen Covey**

> *"No sensible person ever made an apology."*
> **– Ralph Waldo Emerson**

> *"If you ever dream of beating me, you'd better wake up and apologize."*
> **– Muhammad Ali**

A sincere apology, a timely apology, or a romantic apology can go a long way. What's interesting is, if you respond immediately and impressively, you just might gain loyalty and strengthen a relationship.

Character can be defined not by what happens, but by how you react to what happens. Mistakes and problems are simply opportunities. Opportunities to strengthen relationships.

Chapter 64

ARE YOU LISTENING TO THE DEVIL ON ONE SHOULDER, OR THE ANGEL ON THE OTHER?

Unfortunately, shady ethics and wavering morals in both business and relationships are a fact of life. From misleading advertising, to the fudging of a resumé, to taking advantage of a given situation. Driven by greed, desperation, or fierce competition, sometimes in life there is simply a temptation to do the... not-so-right thing.

Just to make a buck.

I learned this early lesson on business ethics when I was 16...

I was suddenly awakened before school one morning by a call from my best friend, whose name was Bart. Bart had just finished working the overnight shift at the corner drugstore, and said in a speedy, sinister voice: *"Come pick me up from work RIGHT now, but pull around to the back and open-up your hatchback."*

I said, *"WHAT?"*

He said, *"Just TRUST ME, now hurry up!!"*

Bewildered, I arrived behind the drugstore within 10 minutes and opened up my hatchback—where Bart proceeded to chuck case after case of CANDY BARS into my trunk.

I inquired *"Dude—WHAT IS GOING ON? What are you doing?"*

"*Just trust me,*" he said with a villainous grin, as he continued stuffing my car with stocking stuffers.

"*BART—COME ON, what's the deal or I'm not driving anywhere. Is this stuff STOLEN???*"

"*NO!*" He assured me. "*It's NOT stolen, now let's GO!!*"

I've never seen so many cases of candy in my LIFE. My trunk wouldn't even close—it was like Willy Wonka's Chocolate Factory on wheels!

So, we raced to school and popped-open the hatchback of my 1980 Chevrolet Citation, which was a MAJOR chick-magnet, by the way. We began furiously selling every candy bar possible before school, at lunch, and afterschool for outrageously low prices. First, five for a dollar. Then, TEN for a dollar. It started a FEEDING FRENZY.

We were getting RICH as chocolate pushers!!

As we hurried to sell every bar before the melted chocolate began sticking to my backseat, I finally asked him again: "*OK, look—you gotta tell me now, dude. WHAT IS THE DEAL? The expiration date is still OK on these candy bars. You're SURE they're not STOLEN?*"

"*NO—they're not STOLEN. My manager told me to throw them out,*" Bart said.

"*Why did your manager tell you to throw them out, Bart?*"

"*Well, apparently a few customers complained yesterday because they... well... found BUGS inside the candy.*"

"*WHAT??*" I exclaimed. "*Are you telling me we just sold our entire school 30 cases of CHOCOLATE COVERED BUGS?!?!*"

"*I'll have you know that's a delicacy in some countries,*" he said.

"*Thanks a lot, Bart. Like I haven't gotten my ASS KICKED enough this semester.*"

Fortunately, no one became seriously ill that day—so all's well that ends well. All in an honest day's work.

From that day on, Bart and I had plenty of fun renaming all of our favorite candies. Reese's Peanut Butter Bugs. Buggerfinger.

Jolly Roachers. Milk Bugs. Mr. Goodbug. You name it...

Although, I still cringe at the sound of a Nestlé Crunch bar crunching to this day. That really took the fun out of Halloween.

Seriously, though, I did learn from that experience. Peer pressure, and the pressure to make a buck, force people to make bad decisions in life. I really felt bad thinking *"what if I made someone sick, or gave them the flu bug?"*

Experiencing guilt can positively impact future decisions in similar situations, ensuring we don't make the same mistakes twice.

So, I never sold any food-like items that Bart gave me ever again.

By the way, I never told my Dad that story. He was an exterminator. It would bug him.

Chapter 65

GET THEM TO LOVE YOU

AND YOU CAN GET AWAY WITH (ALMOST) ANYTHING

Bart's wisdom didn't stop with business. His winning philosophies spilled over into relationships, as well. However, I was all ears since he was waaaayyyy more successful with the opposite sex than I was (*he actually got girls to talk to him without having to do their homework*).

Anyway, Bart always gave me this piece of advice with women:

> **"Get them to fall in love with you**
> **and you can get away with anything."**

Albeit WARPED, the concept did stick with me... especially in the world of business, believe it or not.

My Uncle Jerry, a retired postmaster, told me a legendary story of a postman who delivered within rural Missouri. For years and years, he was so friendly and so trusted with his customers, he convinced his entire county route that mail was only scheduled for delivery three days per week—on Mondays, Wednesdays, and Fridays. He then promptly enjoyed Tuesdays, Thursdays, and Saturdays playing golf, watching television, or relaxing by his backyard pool.

Until the day he retired.

Now that's some poor work ethic, even by government employee standards.

A terrific example of managing expectations, I suppose. But perhaps a better example of under-promising and... **under-delivering**.

In most situations, however, people have the power of choice. If customers are dissatisfied, learn of a mistake, or find they have been wronged, customers can choose to leave and find someone else at the drop of a hat.

Dissatisfaction will catch up to us.

Is our relationship with our customers strong enough to absorb it?

There is a reason that some clients fire or switch vendors after one screw-up. There is no loyalty. No relationship. They don't even like their sales or service rep.

Have you or your company ever screwed-up, and the client was mad for a few days, but they stuck with you? Everyone in the office probably said *"Thank God they like us!"*

That's what we're talking about here.

A company I previously worked for once suffered a SLIGHT oversight on a particular promotion. While both Shell and Chevron were our clients, we accidently shipped 500 Shell logo umbrellas to upper management at Chevron, and shipped 500 Chevron logo umbrellas to upper management at Shell.

Oopsy!

No amount of Alka-Seltzer in the world could have settled this gas problem.

Shell, though upset for weeks, stuck with us. Chevron fired us.

We know for a fact the relationship our account rep had with Shell is what saved us.

So, is your relationship with your customer good enough to overcome a major mistake, an argument, or even having to take on a price increase? Are your personal relationships strong enough to overcome a major fight?

Especially in the beginning of relationships, the margin for error is very small—in business, or dating. If you offend the other person, or do something embarrassing, or run over their pet

Chihuahua in the driveway, you are DONE. No phone call back. No apology accepted. No *"It was nice doing business with you."*

You are done.

The greater the relationship which is established—the more they like you—the better chance you have at a second chance. And perhaps even a third or fourth.

Get them to fall in love with you, and you can get away with (*almost*) anything in life. Because eventually, life happens.

I saw that on a bumper sticker once, so I know it's true.

Chapter 66

REPEAT BUSINESS:
KEEP 'EM COMING BACK FOR MORE

I have a great friend named Mike, who is a successful sales manager with a mortgage company. Mike and I have often joked about the similarities between sales and dating. Mike, you see, really *"gets around"* in the dating world, as well as the sales world.

What's always amazed me about Mike is his continued ability to *"get back together"* with women he dated six months prior, or even ten years prior. I've never seen anything like it!

Granted, some of Mike's women make Samantha from *Sex and the City* look like Mother Teresa. However, there is still a principle to be learned, here.

You see, Mike understands the benefits of *"repeat business."* **If you provide someone with an amazing experience, and keep positive communications open, the greater the chance they will be willing to... do business with you later on down the road.**

Ok, we're not going to belabor this point—hopefully you get the picture. It's easier to re-connect with people whom you've already shared a positive experience with, rather than trying to win over new strangers from scratch.

One highly overlooked key to repeat business is the frequency of that repeat business. We not only have to keep 'em coming back, but more often.

So, what can we learn from oil change facilities, dentists, and a leading toothpaste brand that 4 out of 5 dentists recommend?

In the early 1990's, the marketing team for a major toothpaste brand ran an employee contest to create the best idea to sell more toothpaste. Ideas spanned from incentivizing dentists, to marketing toothpaste for dogs, to having Michael Jordan endorse the product.

The winning idea? Also the simplest.

A frontline operations employee suggested the company increase the size of the hole at the end of each toothpaste tube. When people squeeze toothpaste, they apply it the length the toothbrush head, oblivious to the width that is being applied. Increasing the width of the hole by 15% increases the amount of toothpaste squeezed each time by 15%, which in turn creates the need for consumers to buy more toothpaste at an increased rate of 15%.

Who needs Ivy League marketing grads, anyway?

Dentists and oil change facilities both offer models for us to learn from to get those repeat customers back, and often. As you complete each visit, you're either scheduled a next appointment, or are provided with a little sticker in your window of when you should return.

Seamless. Easy. Effective.

In the 1970's and 1980's, it was recommended to get your oil changed every 5,000 miles. Then, it was recommended every 3,000-5,000 miles. Now, it's 3,000 miles. Hmmm...that's funny. Wouldn't technology and ingenuity improve to make things last longer over the past 30 years? Trust me with the inside scoop on this one. This doesn't have to do with auto care. **This has to do with marketing.**

More power to 'em!

Speaking of oil change facilities, I once helped plan a CRM (that's Customer Relationship Management, folks) project for a major car manufacturer. One process was to mail response letters to customers who requested brochures for a particular vehicle. Well, apparently, managers at oil change stores would order these brochures simply as reading material for their guests in the lobby. No problem, except they would enter the name of the oil change store in the "FIRST" and "LAST" name field online. So, here's how the direct mail letter was sent to them:

"Dear Jiffy,
We'd like to thank you and the rest of the Lube family for your
interest in the new XL-250 4x4 Truck."

I'm guessing Jiffy never took advantage of that XL-250 Truck
offer. I don't think that would have made Mrs. Lube very happy.

SPEND THE MOST TIME WITH THOSE MOST IMPORTANT TO YOU

Salespeople are notorious, unfortunately, for being quite poor at time management.

Sales Manager 1: *"So, how many salespeople work for you?"*

Sales Manager 2: *"About half of them."*

According to the *Oxford English Dictionary*, the word "time" is the most commonly spoken noun in the English language. Perhaps that speaks to its level of importance in our lives.

In business, the ideal goal is to spend most of our time with our most important clients. Although, sometimes that's not as easy as it seems.

It's not that we intentionally take our best clients for granted. Often we become so consumed with finding new customers, we ignore current customers. In other situations, we spend most of our time dealing with our smallest, ankle-biting, low profit, complaining accounts.

Are we wasting valuable time which keeps us from coddling our best and most loved customers, whom we want to give pampered attention to? If so, we should either redirect our time, or consider principle #68: *Know When to Cut Your Losses.*

We can also target a concerted effort on who we want to spend the most time in our lives with, as well.

Think of a favorite relative, or an old friend, where you think to yourself: "*Wow, I wish I could spend more time with this person. I really miss hanging out with them and talking with them on the phone. But, everyone is so busy these days... that's just life. Time passes.*"

Now, think of someone in your life that you currently spend time with, but whenever you hang up with them on the phone or walk back in your door, you complain to yourself "*Why do I even TALK to this person? They completely stress me out! They are so negative and draining!!*"

That's when your significant other says "*I don't know, but we're going out with them again next weekend.*"

Great.

There are two types of people in this world: Those that lift people up, and those that bring people down. We have a choice of who we spend our valuable time in life with.

That is, unless we LIVE with them.

We can pick our clients. We can pick our friends, too.

"*You can pick your friends. You can pick your nose. But you can't pick your friends' nose.*"

In case you were wondering, you can't pick your clients' nose, either.

"*What in the HELL are you doing? Get your FRICKIN' FINGER away from my FACE, or you'll be picking your TEETH up off the FLOOR!!*"

Helping out clients with whatever they need only goes so far, I suppose.

Nevertheless, it's easy to get pulled away in so many different directions, from so many different people.

"How did this person drag me into THAT?"

Either you're in charge of your time, or someone else is in charge of your time. Either you control your schedule, or your schedule controls you.

Here is a great time management concept: *Every time you say "YES" to something in your life, you are saying "NO" to everything else. Similarly, every time you say "YES" to someone in your life, you are saying "NO" to everyone else.*

I've always tried to share this concept with women I dated who were very busy and often stressed out (in other words—ALL OF THEM). I helped them relax, put things in perspective, and prioritize what is truly important in life (like spending more time with me).

Author/Trainer Brian Tracy once said: *"If what you are doing at this very moment isn't helping you achieve your goals, it's keeping you from achieving your goals."*

Life is too short.

So, what are we saying "YES" to?

Better yet, *who* are we saying "YES" to?

Hopefully, our most important clients, and our most important loved ones.

Chapter 68

KNOW WHEN TO CUT YOUR LOSSES

In either business or life, sometimes we must look ourselves in the mirror and face tough questions about a bad relationship:

- ☹ Are they complaining too much?
- ☹ Are they costing us too much money?
- ☹ Are they just flat out making us MAD?
- ☹ Are they wasting too much time and effort to even make it worthwhile?
- ☹ Or, PERHAPS—have they started doing business with someone else?

When consulting for clients, I would always review their list of clients using the 80/20 rule, or the *"Pareto Principle,"* which has many important applications in time, life, and business.

80% of a company's revenue derives from *just 20% of its clients.*

80% of a company's resources are applied to *just 20% of its clients.*

80% of a company's HEADACHES come from *just 20% of its clients.*

The bottom 20% of a company's clients consistently seem to soak up more resources, cause more headaches, and gain nowhere near the profitability as the top 20% of clients.

We can target who we want our clients to be. We can also target who we *don't* want our clients to be.

It might just be time to resign that account (as opposed to re-sign that account), so that company resources can be saved, or reapplied towards finding other clients whose profile match the top 20%.

This concept is also known as *"addition by subtraction,"* or a slightly more blunt term called *"Fire Your Customer."*

A good friend of mine, Chris, owned a printing company in St. Louis. She once had a customer that was so cheap, complaining, and abusive—she finally notified him that her company would not produce projects for him anymore.

It's pretty bad when you begin calling your competitors, saying:

"Take my customer, PLEASE."

Not understanding this concept as a stubborn customer, this guy became upset about the idea of another company working on his projects.

It's pretty bad when you must also personally sell your customer on the competition.

"Hey, my competition is GREAT. They do GREAT work for a GREAT price. In fact, THEY are better than WE are! Here is their address. Better yet, just get in the car. I'll drive you there."

Then, Mr. Persistent kept coming back. Every day. Like a bad nightmare.

This reached a point where Chris simply threatened *"Get off my property before I call the cops."*

He didn't, so she did.

It's definitely pretty bad when you need a restraining order to keep customers out of your place of business.

I thought that only happened at Chippendale clubs.

Of course, people don't respond well to being the one who is "cut" in relationships, either. In college, I received about 25 phone calls a day from an ex-girlfriend after a breakup that went like this:

ANDY: *"Hello."*

JEN: *"I hate you!"*

ANDY: *"Sorry, you must have the wrong number."*

Again, please refer to Chapter #69, *Create an Amicable Breakup (Never Burn Bridges)*, on what to do—or not to do—immediately after ending a relationship.

I've always believed that when one door closes, another door opens. But, sometimes you have to be willing to close the first door to allow the second door to open.

Even though it may not seem like it at the time, you are doing the other person a favor by not wasting their time and allowing their 2nd door to open, as well.

With bad relationships in life and in business, making a decision at the crossroads is paramount. The decision is to either right the relationship, or move on. Inaction is the enemy.

Chapter 69

Did you know there is actually a book titled *The Complete Idiot's Guide to the Breakup*? Apparently, none of my ex-girl-friends consulted this guide when devising their escape.

My first-ever breakup ended in a lot of pain.

Literally.

You see, the worst thing that ever happened to me in high school was I got beat up... by a GIRL. Yep, that's right. In fact, it was my girlfriend (*then immediate ex-girlfriend*).

Gentlemen, I'm not sure what traumatic horror stories you've experienced in life, but let me tell you—it doesn't get any worse than THAT. I still have nightmares about the phrase *"STOP—Get her off me!"*

It really wasn't that impressive, though. Remember, I was a skinny DORK in high school. She actually only hit me with one punch. It was a cheap shot, though. Trust me, if I would have seen it coming... I would have run. But, unfortunately, I didn't possess the catlike reflexes I do today. The ER doctors first thought she had broken my orbital bone, and I had blurred vision in my right eye for three weeks.

People always ask me what I did to deserve it. Let's just say she didn't appreciate my sense of humor as people do now (*right*)? I actually ran into her last year, but learned she now goes by the name "Jim."

I guess that explains the right hook.

Nevertheless, from that point on, my goal in life was to not date any woman who was capable if kicking the CRAP out of me. Although, I soon realized that cut down my odds too much, so that pre-requisite was abolished.

Fortunately, my subsequent girlfriends graduated from physical pain to emotional pain in their determined efforts to shatter my self-esteem.

At least most were up-front:

"It's not me, it's you."

Thanks.

When I first moved to South Florida, I began dating someone for three months. Then one Monday morning, I logged on to Microsoft Outlook, only to learn she broke up with me... VIA EMAIL. I mean, seriously. One, two, or three dates—maybe, but three MONTHS?

I suppose I should have seen it coming from her subject line which read *"SUBJECT: On To Bigger And Better Things."*

I lost serious respect for her that day. Yep, a burned bridge with Andy Masters. **If she thinks for a SECOND that I'm going to recommend her to any of my friends, she's got another thing coming.**

Of course, some people aren't quite so *"nice"* when hard feelings come into play.

Hence, the world of mean and vengeful pranks to get back at someone in relationships. Gentlemen, need some ideas? How about purchasing the German dissolving bikini? That's right. As featured as an ultimate revenge gift on *SPIKE TV*, this bikini looks and feels normal, but is made solely of material which dissolves immediately when entering a pool. It's nice to see we're putting today's modern resources and ingenuity to good use.

I have a sneaking suspicion men were behind this.

However, the same company also sells dissolvable male swim trunks. Touché.

Indeed, men are not the only vindictive ones.

In my programs, I've often shown a huge billboard which was displayed in downtown Des Moines, Iowa, from a highly disgruntled wife which read:

> "Dear Steven-
>
> Do I have your attention now?
>
> I know all about her, you dirty, sneaky, immoral, unfaithful, poorly-endowed slimeball. Everything's caught on tape!
>
> > Your soon-to-be Ex-Wife, Emily.
>
> P.S.—I paid for this billboard from our joint bank account."

Well, I suppose I can't criticize her creativity.

Bad breakups can affect your professional life, as well. I learned the hard way that relationship news spreads quickly on the corporate gossip superhighway—Women TALK!

Once after a break-up, I was walking down our corporate hallway, and a female co-worker who knew my ex-girlfriend gave me *"the look."* And, trust me gentlemen—this wasn't the good *"I think you're HOT"* look. It was the bad *"I want to KILL YOU AND RIP OUT YOUR EYEBALLS"* look. In fact, I'm not really sure what the first look looks like.

Lastly, this principle affects how you break-up from a job, as well. **There is a professional way to end ties with a company, client, or vendor—and a not-so-professional way.**

One disgruntled ex-employee of Akimbo Systems, Stephen Barnes, decided to hack into his former employer's IT network for some fun and revenge. He wiped out all email servers, deleted databases, and SPAMMED contact lists.

Pretty funny.

In fact, it was so funny, the judge forgot to laugh. He was sentenced to one year in prison and ordered to pay $54,000 in restitution.

I can just see him intimidating fellow cell mates with that conviction.

"If anyone TOUCHES me, your email is going DOWN when I get outta here!!"

Whether illegal, unprofessional, or disrespectful, it's all called burning bridges. Remember, all of your exes know 250 people on average. As do all of your past clients and co-workers. **So, how do you *"break-up"* with your customers? Will they ever want to come back someday? Will they recommend you to others?**

Gaining more enemies than friends will catch up with you, as will a bad reputation, in business and in life.

Chapter 70

CONDUCT A
POST-RELATIONSHIP
EVALUATION

Everyone should truly learn from each relationship, either business or personal. The good, the bad, and the ugly. Then we must take responsibility to continually apply what we've learned, and improve in every area possible.

Certainly, many types of sales and service industries offer exit interviews or surveys to customers and clients who, for whatever reason, chose to stop doing business. Maybe a contract expired, the customer moved away, or the customer left because they were dissatisfied. Such surveys are distributed by physicians, financial reps, IT service firms, etc.

So, I reviewed many of these actual exit interview survey questions, and thought to myself:

"Wouldn't it be great if...?"

Wouldn't it be great if we could use these exact same exit interview questions at the conclusion of our romantic relationships? That would be valuable feedback.

It would go something like this:

OVERALL RELATIONSHIP

1) *"How did you hear about me?"*

2) *"Were you satisfied with the communication and feedback during the relationship?"*

3) *"Do you feel you were treated with courtesy and respect throughout the relationship?"*

4) *"Do you feel you received as much attention and personal contact as you desired?"*

5) *"Do you feel your needs were met?"*

SERVICES PROVIDED

1) *"Were services performed to the level of satisfaction as promised?"*

2) *"What services did you benefit from most often?"*

3) *"Were you satisfied with the speed of service?"*

4) *"Were you satisfied with the frequency of service?"*

5) *"Were you satisfied with the responsiveness to your after-hours needs?"*

6) *"Were you satisfied with the innovative techniques that were utilized?"*

7) *"Were you satisfied with the tools and technology utilized?"*

8) *"Did you also use the services of anyone else during the relationship?"*

9) *"If so, whose services did you prefer? Why?"*

10) *"Was your dissatisfaction in this area why you decided to leave?"*

MOVING FORWARD

1)   *"Do you know of anyone else who could benefit from my services?"*

2)   *"Are there any pieces of advice you'd like to provide, so that I may service those in the future even better?"*

3)   *"Would you be willing to provide a testimonial so that I may initiate contact with others just like you?"*

4)   *"Would you be willing to let us use photos or videos of your experience for future promotions on the Internet or other print media?"*

5)   *"Would you ever consider doing business with me again?"*

The simple gesture of soliciting feedback shows that we care, and that we appreciated the relationship. **It's always important to continue positive communications, in case a chance exists for another... relationship... in the future.**

Chapter 71

STAY POSITIVE
AND BOUNCE BACK
AFTER DISAPPOINTMENTS

In the 1994 comedy *Dumb and Dumber*, lovable loser Lloyd Christmas, played by Jim Carrey, had this positive outlook:

Lloyd: *"Come on, give it to me straight. I drove a long way to see you, the least you can do is level with me. What are my chances?"*

Mary: *"Not good."*

Lloyd: *"You mean not good, like one out of a hundred?"*

Mary: *"I'd say more like one in a million."*

Lloyd: *"So, you're telling me there's a chance!"*

Hall of Fame Manager Whitey Herzog was once asked about his disappointment of losing twice in the World Series, while only winning it once. He replied: *"I'd rather be 1 out of 3, than 0 out of 0."*

Funny, that's quite similar to the old saying:

"It is better to have loved and lost, than to have never loved at all."

We've all had to deal with losses, failures, and disappointments. Losing clients. Losing jobs. Losing loved ones. We've all had to deal with *"the one that got away."*

I was on a cruise ship once with a few down-on-their-luck friends, and was doing my best to cheer up the sorry saps by spouting ridiculous humor at every turn. My friend Mario began to hit me whenever I shared another one of my dumb jokes, since I was apparently going "*overboard*" with all of my stupid puns (pardon the pun).

The gang conversed late into the evening one night, mostly complaining about women, relationships, and rejection. But we awakened early for a fresh day of adventure, and my purpose was to serve as the eternal optimist for everyone.

Mario yelled: "*Masters—Why the hell are you spending so much time fixing your hair? We're going scuba diving in the ocean for crying out loud!*"

I smiled and said: "*Yeah, but there are a lot of fish in the sea!*"

He punched me.

Twice.

A wise pastor shared this statement with me after a funeral once. He said **"The human spirit is resilient."** At our lowest moments of loss, grief, rejection, failure, or embarrassment—we see no light, no hope. Then, after a few moments, or a few hours, or perhaps even days or weeks, there is light. The human spirit is wired to offer us hope that our brightest day just might come after our darkest night.

In addition to seeing humor in almost everything, I also try to stay positive by *"keeping things in perspective."* Sometimes the world helps me out.

One afternoon I was enduring a long layover in the Atlanta airport, and began chit-chatting with a fellow standing next to me in a lengthy food line. Suddenly, I reached for my leg and grimaced slightly. The guy said "*What's wrong?*"

I replied: "*Awww... I strained my calf last night in a freak billiards accident, so it really hurts—especially if I have to bend over or walk up stairs. It has NOT been a good last 24 hours, let me put it that way.*"

That's the exact moment I turned to see the customer behind me in a wheelchair with no legs at all. He was in military gear.

I didn't even feel worthy to look him in the eye. I've never felt so small in my life.

Who am I? A bad day for me is getting stuck in traffic. A bad day for him is getting stuck in traffic, in Baghdad, when a suicide car bomb explodes. Who am I to complain about a frickin' bad day?

Most of us think we're having a bad day when the printer jams. Most of us think we're having a bad day when it's raining and we can't find a taxi. Most of us don't know what a bad day is.

Keeping life's challenges in perspective is the first step to bouncing back quickly and staying positive. Most of our failures and disappointments really aren't as bad as they might seem at the time. In fact, with most we can look back and laugh about shortly thereafter.

"Tragedy plus time equals comedy."
– Woody Allen

Chapter 72

GAIN HOPE FROM SUCCESS STORIES OF OTHERS

We all need heroes to help inspire us in life, and help us believe in ourselves. Like the father who shared this motivational quip with his son:

SON: *"I'll never be famous like them, Dad. I'm just a nobody."*

DAD: *"Son, always remember this: Everybody who's a somebody started out as a nobody. Just like you."*

I've always believed witnessing success stories of others can either be discouraging, or encouraging. Hence, these examples:

SUCCESS STORIES THAT ARE DISCOURAGING

Relationships

When I was a freshman in high school, the girl I had a major crush on surprisingly chose the MUSCLE-BOUND QUARTERBACK OF THE VARSITY FOOTBALL TEAM WHO DROVE A CORVETTE TO SCHOOL over me. *"I will NEVER be like him. I'll never get a girl like that."*

Business

When I first began speaking professionally, I bought tickets to a major motivational seminar at a 20,000-seat arena in St. Louis. I saw ultra-talented international speaker Krishna Dalvi for the first time. He was SO funny, SO inspirational, and had such amazing content, I literally almost quit as a speaker. *"I will NEVER be that good. I'm in the wrong profession. This guy blows me away."*

SUCCESS STORIES THAT ARE ENCOURAGING

Relationships

When I was in high school, a friend once told me I should gain motivation from seeing beautiful girls with DORKS. From that moment on, whenever I saw a beautiful girl in the mall with a dork, I was inspired. *"If THAT guy can get a girl like that, then I've got a chance!!"*

Business

When I began speaking professionally, I had a mentor who told me *"you will gain motivation from successful speakers who AREN'T THAT GOOD."* From that moment on, I saw so many successful speakers who were sooooo boring, with stale content. That inspired me. *"If THAT guy can make it, I KNOW I can!!"*

Common lesson: **You don't have to be the best to succeed. You simply have to be better than the worst who do.** (I'm sure I won't win any motivational awards with that quote).

There have been millions of men over the past 50 years who might have been discouraged watching women swoon over stars from Elvis to Brad Pitt. FORGET THEM. If Barney Fife and Screech can get action, we've all got a chance. Heck, even Gilligan got to make out with Mary Ann in one episode, and Mary Ann was HOT.

Lastly, this concept reminds me of the story of two guys getting chased by a bull. One guy turns confidently to the other and says, *"I don't have to outrun the bull, I just have to outrun YOU."*

Tony Robbins once said *"Success leaves clues."*

210

Maybe it's the number one salesperson in your organization. Or, maybe it's the unattractive dork with a beautiful girlfriend in the mall. **Both are doing something right.**

So, what is it?

I bet both possess confidence in the positives they have to offer. I bet both know how to make people laugh. I bet both understand how to develop a relationship. I bet both know how to make other people feel special.

None of these qualities are unreachable for any of us. In fact, they are in all of us.

Chapter 73

UNDERTAKE GOAL SETTING, NOT GOAL SETTLING

I believe we are conditioned to set our goals too low in life.

You see, if we set goals that are really, really high—in anything—we increase the chance that we might fail. No one likes to fail, and no one likes to disappoint others or look stupid when we fail. So, we readjust our goals down to a much more *"realistic and attainable"* level.

We do this in business, career, and even relationships. It's why men don't ask the most beautiful girl to prom, but rather opt for a much "safer" pick whom we believe will say "Yes."

This also reminds me of the motto for desperate single guys on a late evening out: *"If she doesn't meet your standards, lower your standards."*

Many people call setting objectives which are *"realistic and attainable"* goal setting. I call it *"goal settling."* This is how most people fail to reach their superstar potential—in anything. When you lower your goals in life, you lower your accomplishments.

Your accomplishments in life are in direct correlation with your expectations in life.

What if someone would have told Benjamin Franklin to set *"realistic and attainable"* goals? Or Oprah Winfrey? Or Barack Obama? Expect everything with all of your heart and mind, and you'll get it.

Sam Walton once said:

"High expectations are the key to everything."

Donald Trump once said:

"If you're going to think anyway, think big."

Ayn Rand once said:

"The question isn't 'Who's going to let me?'
It's 'Who's going to stop me?'"

I developed a concept in one of my programs called *"Million-dollar goal setting."* Take any goal that someone might have. Perhaps it's writing a book, running a marathon, starting a company, increasing sales by 50%, or earning a 4.0 GPA in college. If someone gave you $1,000,000 to complete that goal in one year, could you do it? I bet you could, right? Then, you're telling yourself it IS possible. It IS achievable. **You have the potential to do it.**

Forget *"realistic and attainable."* Create your goals high enough that if someone gave you $1,000,000, you could achieve it. Impossible is nothing.

So, how do we define success in dating and relationships? What's the goal?

I once had someone after a program ask me that if I was such an expert on dating, why was I still single? Hahaha... Fair enough question to ponder, I suppose.

So, does that mean success in relationships is getting married?

If so, some of my friends are so successful at this stuff, they've been married TWICE already. They must be GOOD!!

Further, if dating success is defined as one who gets married, then one who gets married even quicker than everyone else

must really know what they are doing. We should all look to the female who only had one boyfriend in her life and married him at age 18. She was 1-for-1. She didn't have any unsuccessful dates at all... she NAILED it. Wow, she must be an expert on dating!

Let's just stick with the idea that success can be defined by the goals that one sets for oneself.

As documented in the popular book and DVD *The Secret*, I do believe in the proven principle of visualizing your goals, whatever your goals may be. Print out a picture of you on the beach, you with your new business, you driving your dream car, etc. *The Law of Attraction* and the power of visualizing your goals has helped create success and happiness for millions throughout history.

Certainly, this concept also works in dating and relationships. Although, gentlemen, be careful not to take this concept of visualizing too far, such as taping pictures of *Playboy* centerfolds all over your ceiling. Laugh, but I had an ex-roommate who did that. To protect the names of the guilty, I'll just call him by his first name: RICKY...YOU KNOW WHO YOU ARE!!

FOCUS ON PERSONAL DEVELOPMENT TO BE THE BEST YOU CAN BE

I've always been obsessed with taking something, and making it better—whether it be individuals or organizations. Hence, one of my graduate degrees was in Human Resources Development, and the name of my company is **Masters Performance Improvement**.

By the way, with that company title, you wouldn't believe how many people have asked if I was a sex therapist.

"No, but I am willing to listen."

Always strive to become better at your craft. Read *"How To"* books. Attend seminars. Subscribe to trade magazines. Keep up-to-date on how technology, or the economy, affects your job or industry. Network with colleagues to gain real advice and tips, not just to gain new contacts to help find your next client (or next job).

Find a mentor.

Find someone who has *"been there, done that."* Find someone who has experienced successes that you would like to experience. Find someone who can help show you the right and wrong way to do things.

Like my best friend from high school, Bart.

Always ask yourself:

What can I do to become better?

What can I do to truly help my company become better?

Why did I lose that last boyfriend/girlfriend?

Why did I lose that last client?

Why did I lose that last pair of sunglasses?

Besides *Rocky*, I'm not a big fan of "chick flicks." However, the 2003 film *How to Lose a Guy in 10 Days* with Matthew McConaughey and Kate Hudson was just fabulous. Why? If you want two hours of stress-free sales/service training, replace one word in the title and view the film as *How to Lose a Client in 10 Days*.

You'll achieve the same results from applying the same actions in the movie. Being selfish. Dishonest. Smothering. Annoying. Giving others more attention. Pleading for him to be the father of your children.

None of these are effective with clients, either.

We've all seen those magazine features in line at the grocery store, such as *101 Ways to Keep the Fire in Your Romance*, right?

These articles are usually just to the left of that month's Brad and Angelina photo. Most are basically the same flavor of article recycled each month, but can offer nice tips and reminders for me—I mean us. Relationships take effort and focus, especially to keep them healthy, fresh, and thriving.

Exercise, and live a healthy lifestyle. Working out can be a stress reliever, and actually provides people with more energy. It can also make you feel better about yourself, which in turn makes you feel more confident, more approachable, and more attractive to the opposite sex... or potential customers.

I recommend Richard Simmons, personally.

Further, there are the additional appearance helpers such as tanning, getting an in-vogue haircut, and receiving a pampered manicure/pedicure to make you look and feel your absolute best. Then, there lies the final level for the ambitious appearance-obsessed types, which includes botox, liposuction, eye-lift, tummy-tuck, and... coming from down here in trendy

South Florida... I'd be remiss not to add the increasingly popular butt implants (*whatever happened to good 'ole fashioned Dunkin Donuts*)?

I must say, it does look wonderful and robust, but I had to buy all new jeans.

No matter our fancy, we should always strive to be the best we can be in our work and personal lives.

Chapter 75

CELEBRATE YOUR SUCCESSES
(STOP AND SMELL THE DOZEN ROSES)

Small celebrations in life include enjoying that extra dessert, shopping for a new outfit at the mall, or taking a day off to experience one of our favorite activities. I'm also a big fan of BIG celebrations, personally. So, certainly, *make those vacations happen!* It's refreshing for both life and career.

Or, at least it's supposed to be.

I once took a trip with a girlfriend to a resort in Playa del Carmen, Mexico, hoping for some celebration, relaxation, and romance. The first day was mostly cloudy, so I skipped the sunscreen and decided to lube-up with a heaping palm full of tanning accelerator instead.

As a fair-skinned blonde guy, that proved to be a bigger mistake than tossing my spandex off, before learning this WASN'T a nude beach (*I'm still upset about the Grandma who pulled her binoculars out*).

I was LOBSTER RED from head to toe, with the worst case of sun poisoning on my feet, which swelled to an unbelievable, literally football-like size. I looked like some clown with big floppy red feet, missing only a big purple nose and curly yellow wig to match. For the next six days, I laid on my back in bed and stared at the ceiling.

Miserable.

But, hey, at least my girlfriend had a great time going to the beach every day without me. THANKS FOR THE SUPPORT.

The last evening of the trip, I challenged myself to attend this semi-formal dinner at the nicest restaurant in the resort. I wore loose pants, a loose shirt—and waddled my way across the resort with no shoes or socks. I was moving slower than a turtle with two broken legs.

I finally approached the front of the line to enter. The maitre d' pointed at the sign and said *"Sorry, Señor—Must have shoes."*

That's when he glanced down at my feet, and started LAUGHING UNCONTROLLABLY. He turned and yelled something in Spanish to his amigo in the kitchen, which could be loosely translated into *"Hey, Jose—Get over here and check out this DORK TOURIST IDIOT!"*

Then the rest of the waiters and cooks stopped working, and immediately came over to laugh at the dork tourist. *"HAHAHA-HAHA!!... We've seen a lot of sunburns around here, but nothing like that... HAHAHAHAHA!!... Oh, Señor!!"*

Thanks.

I didn't know the guests were the ones who provided the entertainment for the staff at this resort. Next, I was just waiting for the PA announcement overhead: *"All resort employees please report at once to the El Diablo restaurant to come see the freak show."*

"You can go on in, sir," the maitre d' finally said with a condescending pity in his voice. *"I will seat you near the front in the VIP section."* As I mentioned in Chapter 47, sympathy works sometimes.

To be allowed to board the flight back home, I had to buy size 14 flip-flops from the airport gift shop. The straps hurt so bad, I had to go to the bathroom and wrap toilet paper around them.

Yeah, I was really lookin' GQ then.

I will never forget this teenage girl who sat across from me in the airport terminal as we waited to board our flight. She just kept staring at me and COULD NOT STOP LAUGHING.

"So, you think this is really funny, huh? It'll be even more funny when I UNWRAP THIS PUSS-FLOWING TOILET PAPER FROM MY FEET TO WIPE THAT STUPID SMILE OFF YOUR FACE."

Ok, Ok... I didn't say that. I found humor in it, too, I suppose.

About 6 years later.

Nevertheless, I was actually refreshed when I returned to the office the next week, after my doctor assured me that amputation wouldn't be necessary.

As the old saying goes, a bad week on vacation is better than a good week at work.

I guess.

Chapter 76

HAVE FUN!

Love what you do, every day.

Write down the Top 10 things you love about your company, your job, or your significant other, and keep the list on your desk. **Go see** stand-up comedians. **Watch** your favorite band or musician in concert. **Take that dream vacation** to Mexico (*please apply sunscreen liberally*).

Think about one city or country in the world that you want to visit before you die, and **book the tickets. Today.** Watch the movie *The Bucket List* with Jack Nicholson and Morgan Freeman, and become inspired to go skydiving and eat lunch under the Eiffel Tower.

Spend 15 minutes or less, and 15 dollars or less, on yourself.

What if you applied just 1/100th of your time towards that fun project or hobby you haven't gotten around to? What could you enjoy this week? What could you accomplish this year? Or, tomorrow?

As part of my favorite exercise in my work-life balance program, I challenge people to brainstorm as many wishes as they can in one minute, where they've ever said this to themselves: *"I've always wanted to do that... I know I need to start doing that... I would be so happy if I could spend time doing that!"* Participants fill this "START BOX" with all of these wonderful, happy, rewarding, and fulfilling items. But, of course, there's no way to start these things, because everyone is just way too busy these days. But, maybe someday.

However, for most people, someday never comes.

Next, we complete this 25-minute exercise on where we truly spend our time, where we waste our time, and where we'd rather spend our time. Then, we commit 1/100th of our time to START doing anything in that START box we want to do.

An amazing thing happens when we actually start things in our START box. We get excited. We get on a roll. We get our adrenaline pumping. This triggers a DOMINO EFFECT, and we realize how excited we are finally applying time to...........!!!

Fifteen minutes per day turns into 45 minutes per day. One hour on a weekend turns into 3 or 4 hours on a weekend. Each of us possess the ability, and the time, to accomplish or enjoy anything in our START box.

I love receiving responses from people around the country who have taken just the first simple step with something great in their START BOX. One day I received this email from a previous audience attendee:

"I also wanted to update you that I accomplished one of my goals. I have always wanted a convertible and the practical part of me had always won out when I have bought Toyota Camry's and Honda Accords... not anymore! I am proud to say that I bought a black BMW 330ci convertible 2 weeks ago and every time I see it, I grin from ear to ear. Now, driving it is another story... every time I see a Honda Accord... I downshift into 4th and Mario Andretti their practical *ss!"

Mark Twain once said:

"Twenty years from now, you will be more disappointed by the things you didn't do, than the things you did."

Having fun and living life is contagious. If you write two pages per week for 52 weeks, you have your first 104-page book. Sign up for those guitar lessons. Sign up for that day at the spa. Go jump out of a plane. And, don't rule out that Wet T-Shirt Contest, either.   ;)

Chapter 77

THE ULTIMATE GOAL: BUILDING A LONG-TERM RELATIONSHIP

Life is truly about relationship building. Not experiencing thousands of short-term relationships where people pass in and out of our lives, but sustaining mutually beneficial long-term relationships.

The themes of this book lead to success in building relationships in both business and our personal lives. Developing relationships takes investing time, effort, and creativity.

> *It's about making the other person feel special and appreciated, such as delivering **a dozen roses, when it's not Valentine's Day.***
>
> *It's about having fun and making people laugh and smile, such as delivering **an autographed baseball on a first date.***
>
> *It's about spending 15 minutes or less, with 15 dollars or less, to make an amazing impact on people's lives, such as **sending a case of A&W Root Beer to a client's home.***

If we focus on the other person, and truly work to build long term-relationships in our lives, then we can become happy and successful with any endeavor.

I once was scheduled to present a program in Prescott, Arizona. My girlfriend at the time had never seen the Grand Canyon, so I decided to bring her along with me. I did some research, and decided to plan a romantic surprise for her at sunset on the South Rim of the Grand Canyon.

223

Unfortunately, we got off to a late start driving in from Phoenix that morning, which is about five hours away from the Grand Canyon. I was trying to rush along the way, but I also didn't want to let her in on the surprise. Well, you know women... bathroom break here, stop for a photo there, shop for some souvenirs... COME ON!!! My chances of making it to the Grand Canyon by sunset were literally growing dimmer by the minute.

Suddenly, we curved around a bend, and witnessed the most spectacular view we had ever seen in our lives. It was the approach towards Sedona, Arizona, surrounded by stunning red rock mountains.

It looked like a brilliant artist had painted the most magnificent mural ever, and used the sky as his canvas.

So, we decided to slow down and take in the surroundings. We stumbled upon the *"Chapel of the Holy Cross,"* which was actually built into the side of a mountain which overlooked the valley.

Taken by the moment, my despair for not making the Grand Canyon on time was calmed by the splendor of our view.

Then I remembered one of my favorite quotes from Dr. Martin Luther King, Jr., who once said:

"The time is always right to do the right thing."

So, I got down on one knee, handed her that romantic surprise, and asked her to marry me.

She said *"Yes."*

By the way, remember the first date whom I told *"You're even more breathtaking than the chicken fingers?"*

That was her. She's on the book cover with me.

Told 'ya I had her from that moment on.   ;)

On May 9, 2009, my breathtaking bride Laurie and I were happily married on Miami Beach, Florida.

HONORABLE MENTIONS

1. Be a GREAT Communicator
2. Always Be Working Towards a Common Goal
3. Common Courtesy (*Not Always that Common*)
4. Cope with Getting Stood Up
5. The Grass is Always Greener on the Other Side
6. Always Be Looking for that Next HOT Prospect
7. Are You Shooting for Quantity or Quality?
8. Don't Hate the Player, Hate the Game
9. Deal with Awkward Run-Ins with Exes
10. Looks Aren't Everything
11. Have the Ability to Put Out Fires Quickly
12. Follow Proper Protocol and Etiquette
13. Be Available 24 Hours a Day, 7 Days a Week ;)
14. When Past Relationships Haunt You!
15. Product Life Cycle (*Intro, Growth, Maturity, Decline!*)
16. Money Talks
17. Have a Mentor
18. Image is Everything
19. But Wait, There's More! (*Always Keep Adding Value*)
20. Practice Patience and Understanding
21. Surround Yourself with a Supportive Team
22. Reasons Why Relationships Fail are the Same
23. You Don't Know What You've Got Until It's Gone

If you liked this book, I would love to hear from you.
Please drop me a line at andy@andy-masters.com,
or catch me on Facebook or Twitter.
If you didn't like this book,
you probably didn't get this far anyway,
so it doesn't matter.

MORE INFO ON
BOOKS AND PROGRAMS
BY ANDY MASTERS

For speaking availability or volume book discounts for
your event or organization, contact Andy's office directly,
or visit his website: http://www.andy-masters.com.

Thank you!